Southern Gospel Piano
Joyful Gospel

Darrell Archer

PREFACE

"Now faith is the substance of things hoped for, the evidence of things not seen"
Hebrews 11:1

Faith is what has enabled the Christian believer to accomplish the impossible over seemingly insurmountable odds. Misplaced faith leads to disappointment, but faith in God and in His Son, Jesus Christ leads to abundant life.

Down through the years, the faith of those who follow Christ has been expressed through the playing and singing of hymns and gospel songs. The pilgrims who first set foot on the shores of their new homeland prayed and sang a hymn and the gospel singing has continued until this very day.

The power of the Gospel Song to reach out and touch people right where they are cannot be overestimated. Too many lives have been transformed to truthfully state anything to the contrary.

Gospel means "good news," so it is no surprise that many songs of faith are joyful, rhythmic, exciting, upbeat, and lively.

This collection of lively gospel piano arrangements offers the keyboardist the opportunity of presenting songs that are sure to be readily accepted, instantly recognized, and greatly appreciated. While playing through these carefully chosen selections, be sure to remember the message behind each composition, and God's love will be conveyed not only to you but to those listening.

Table of Contents

Life is Like a Mountain Railroad

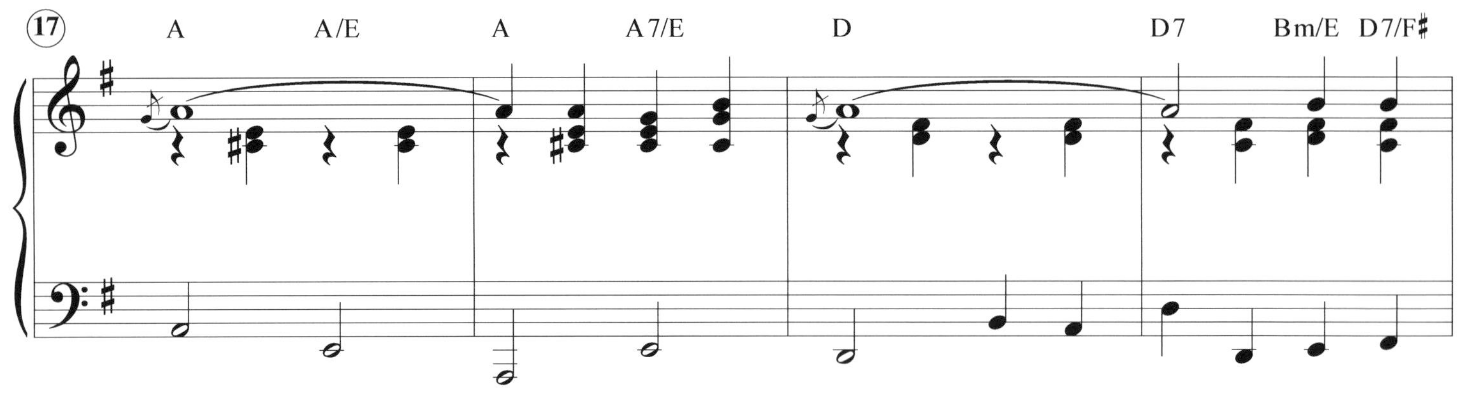
17
A   A/E   A   A7/E   D   D7   Bm/E D7/F#

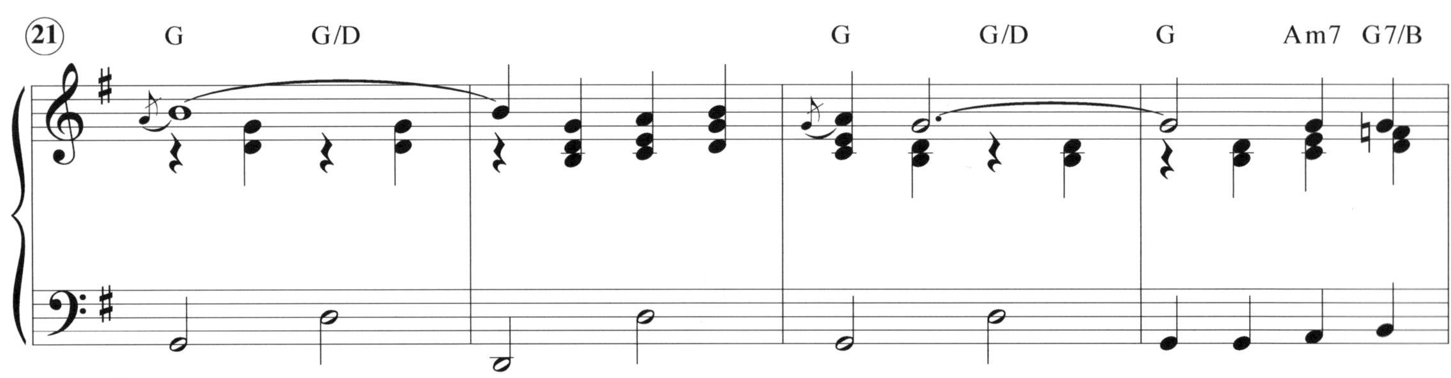
21
G   G/D   G   G/D   G   Am7 G7/B

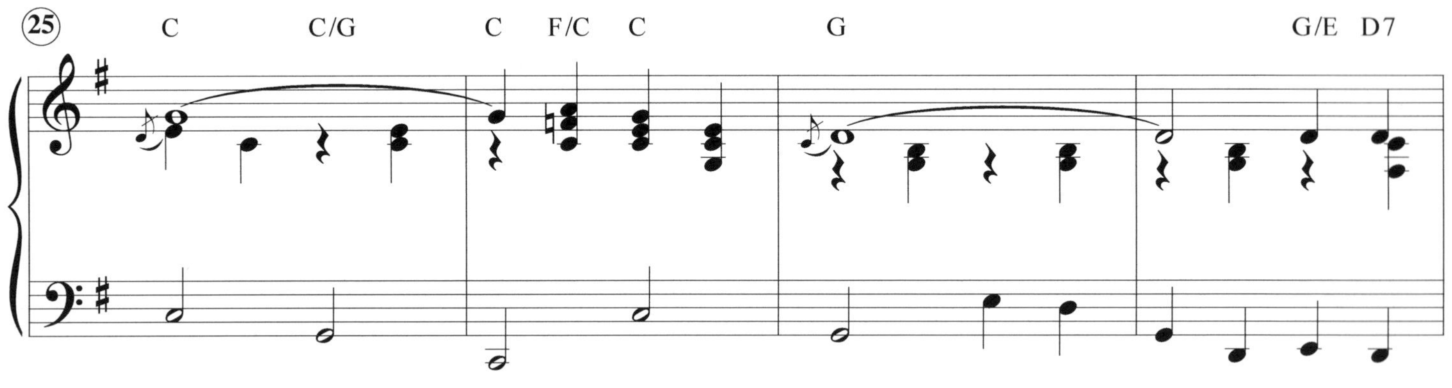
25
C   C/G   C   F/C C   G   G/E D7

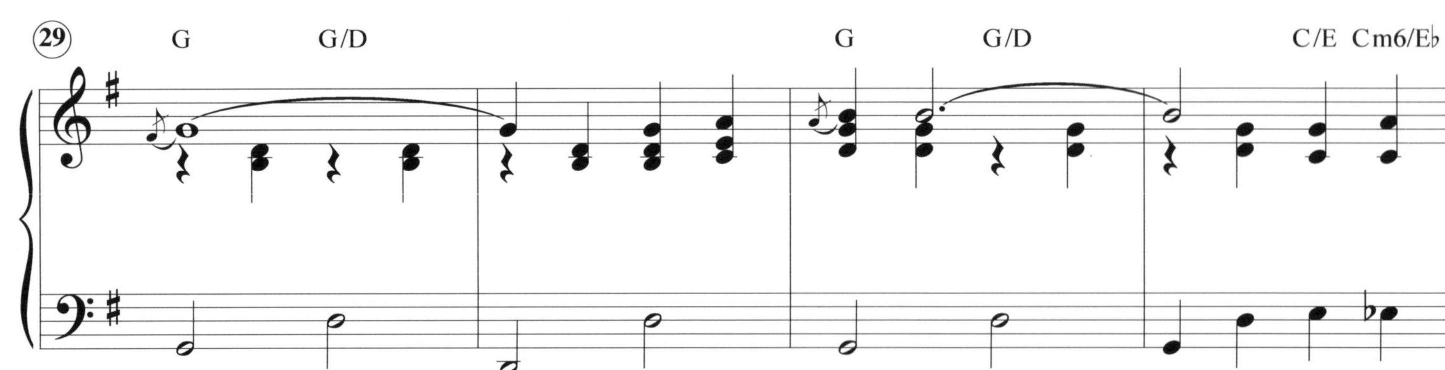
29
G   G/D   G   G/D   C/E Cm6/Eb

33
G G/E G/B G/D D D7 G G/D G N.C.
f
37
C C/G C Cm6 G G/D G
41
Bm7/F# Em A 7/C# D A7 D D7/F#
45
G Bm G7/D G7 D/A G7/B C C/G C C/E Cm6/Eb

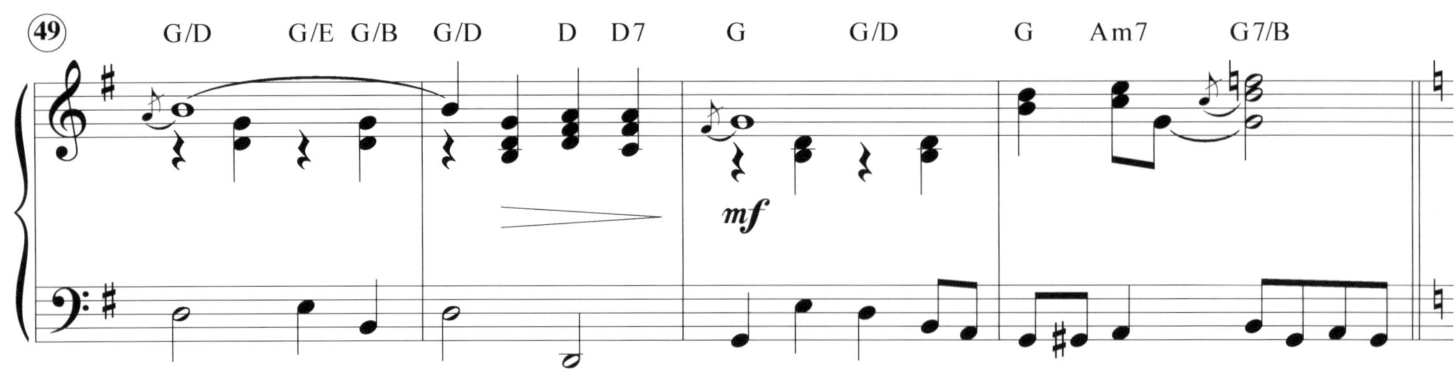
49
G/D   G/E G/B   G/D   D   D7   G   G/D   G   Am7   G7/B
mf

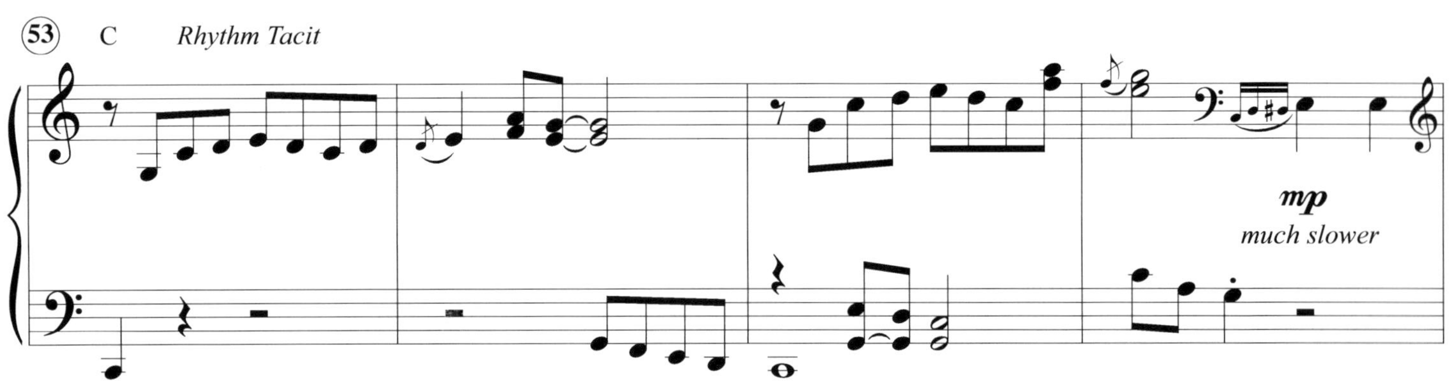
53   C   Rhythm Tacit
mp
much slower

57
L.H.
p
R.H.
L.H.

61
65
69
8va
mf
8va bassa

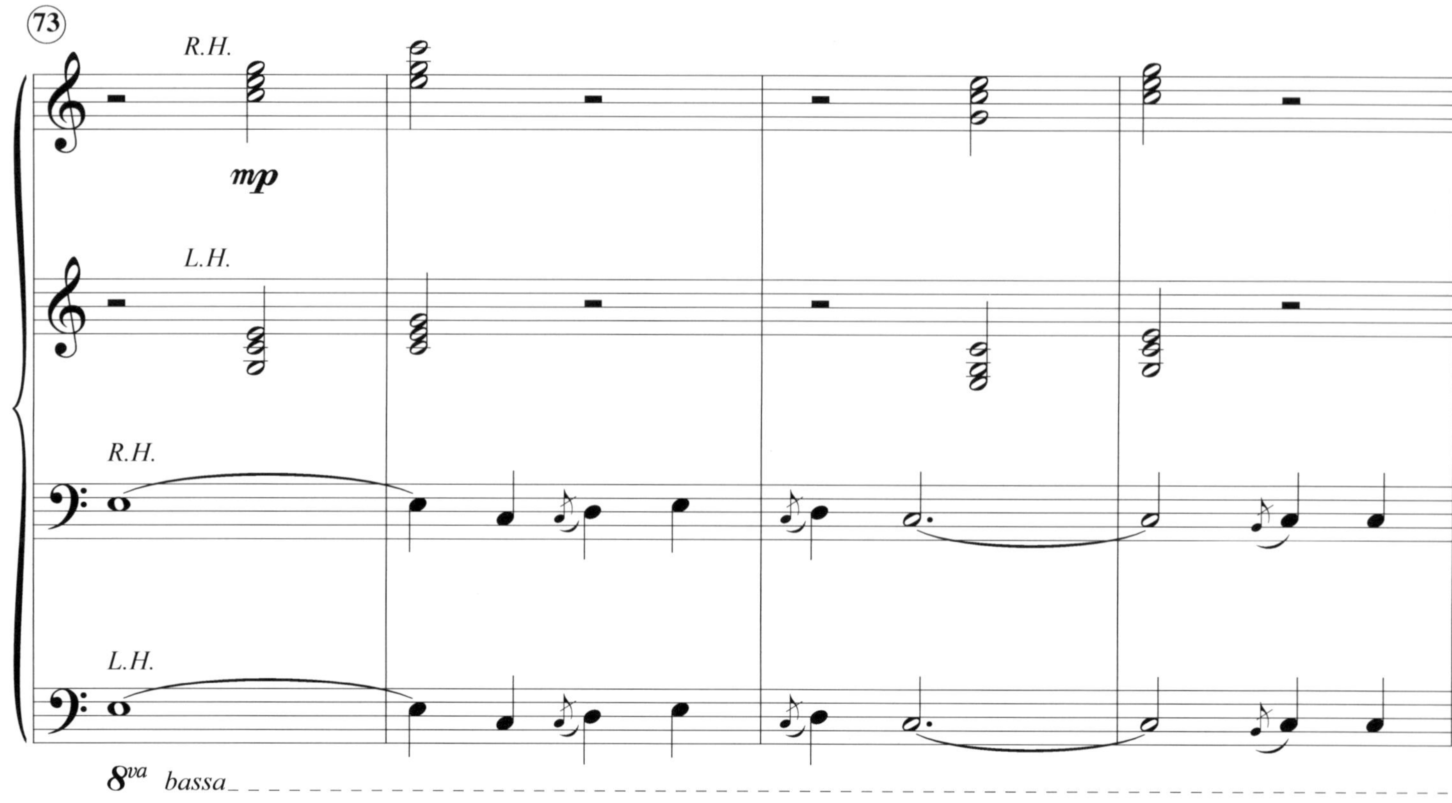
73
R.H.
mp
L.H.
R.H.
L.H.
8va bassa

77
8va bassa

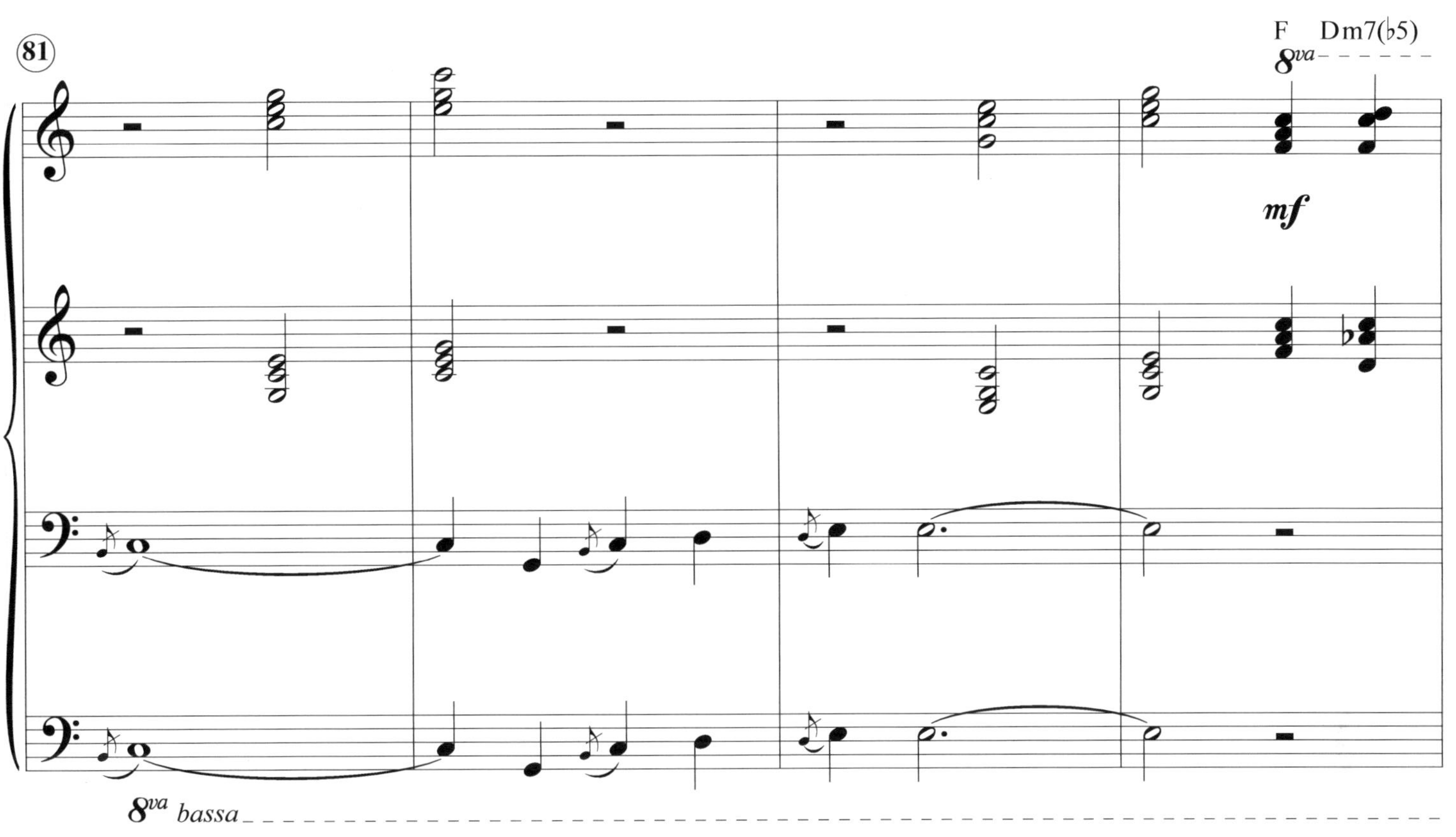
81
F   Dm7(♭5)
8va
mf
8va bassa

85
C
(8va)
G7
C
N.C.
f   a tempo
mp
accel.
8va bassa

F
F/A
Fm6/A♭
101
C/G
C/A
C/E
C/G
G
E7/G♯
Am
Am/G
Am/E
Fm
Fm/D
B♭9
poco a poco rit. e dim.
105
C
C/E
C/F
C/F♯
C/G
G7/A
G7/B
C
C/G
C
molto rit.
p

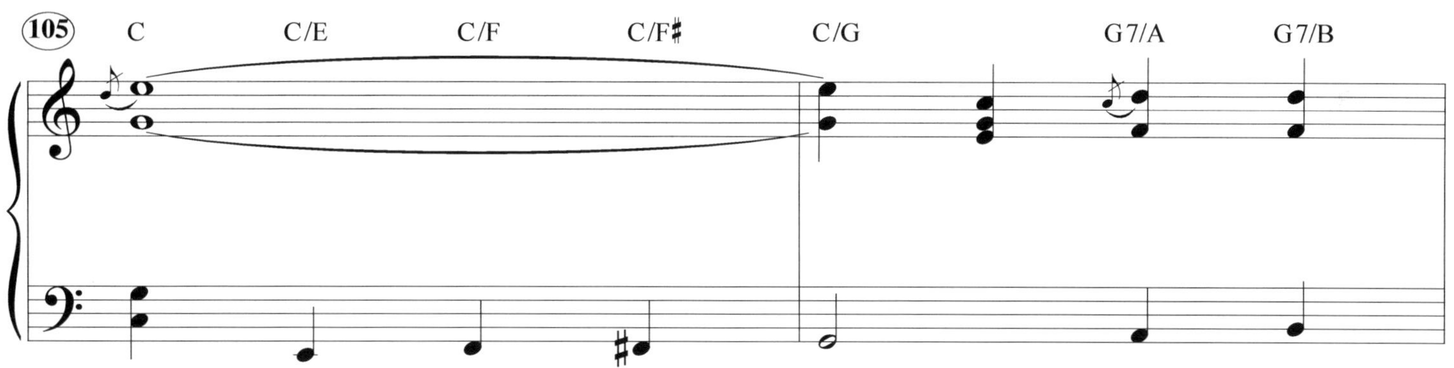

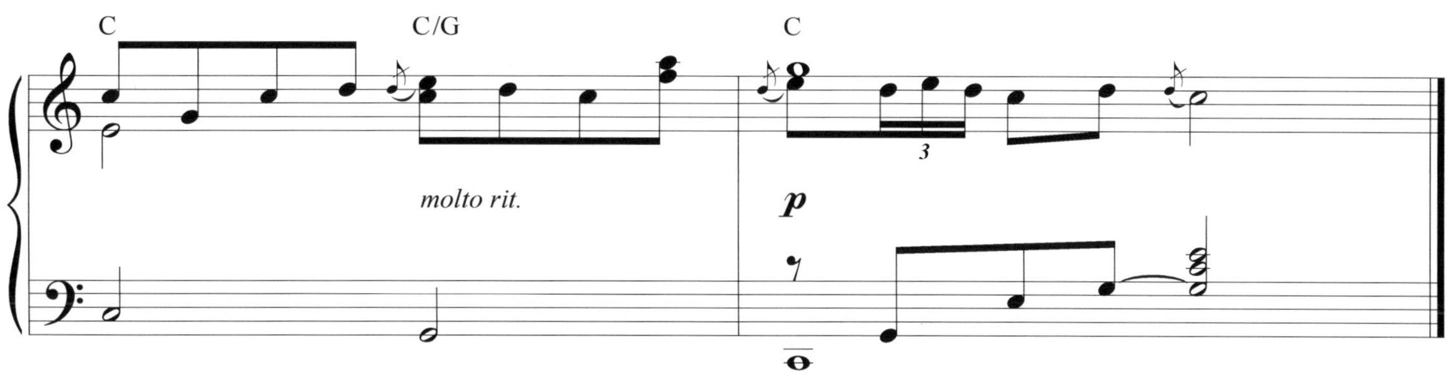

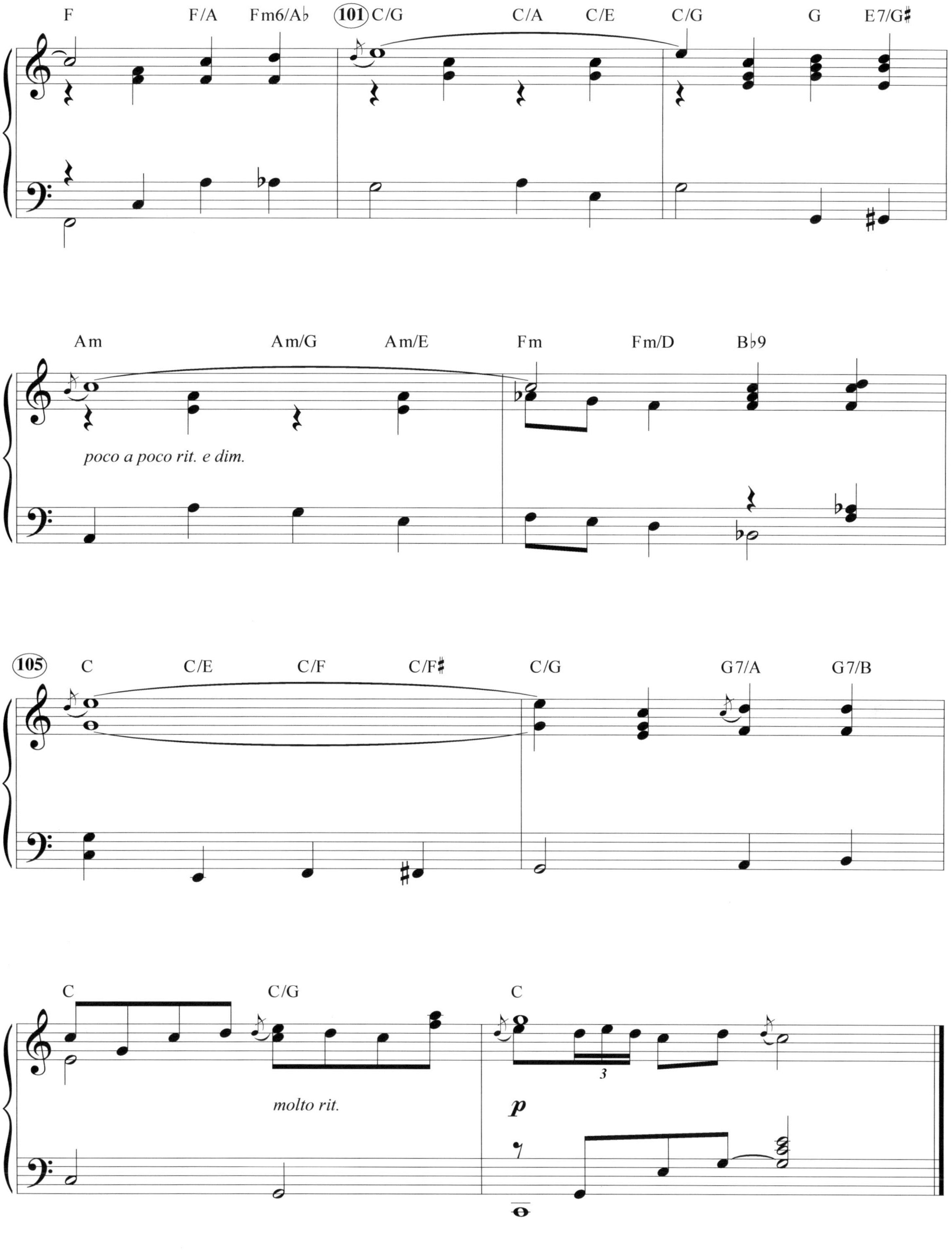

Nothing but the Blood

Nothing but the Blood

Nothing but the Blood
D7/A D7 G/G F/E G/D 35 C
f
Am7 G C 39
mp f
Am7 G C C7
mp
43 F Fsus F F△7 F6 F C Csus
p

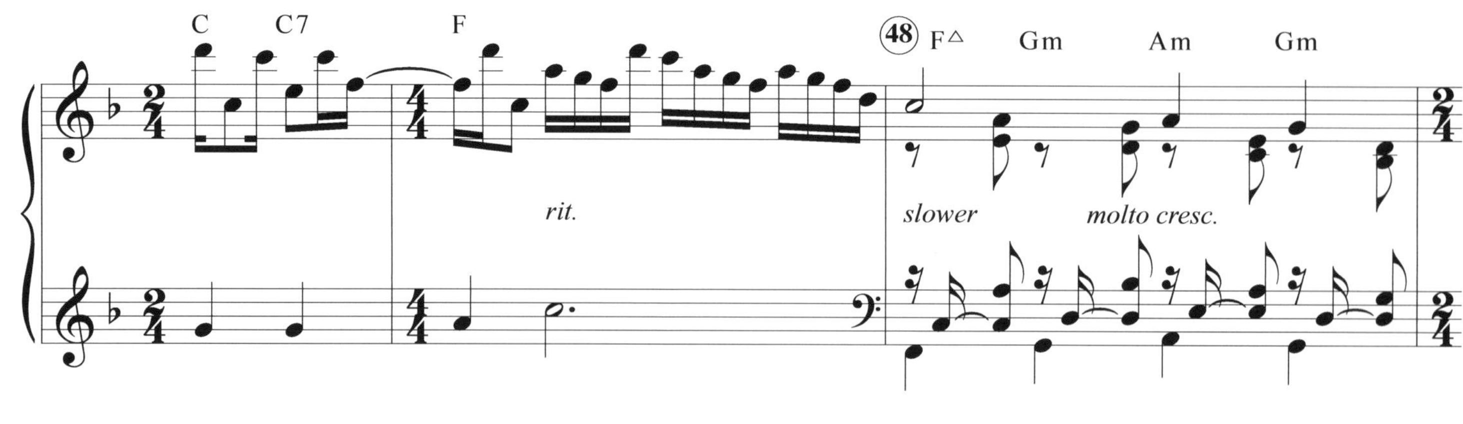
C   C7   F
48 F△   Gm   Am   Gm
rit.
slower   molto cresc.

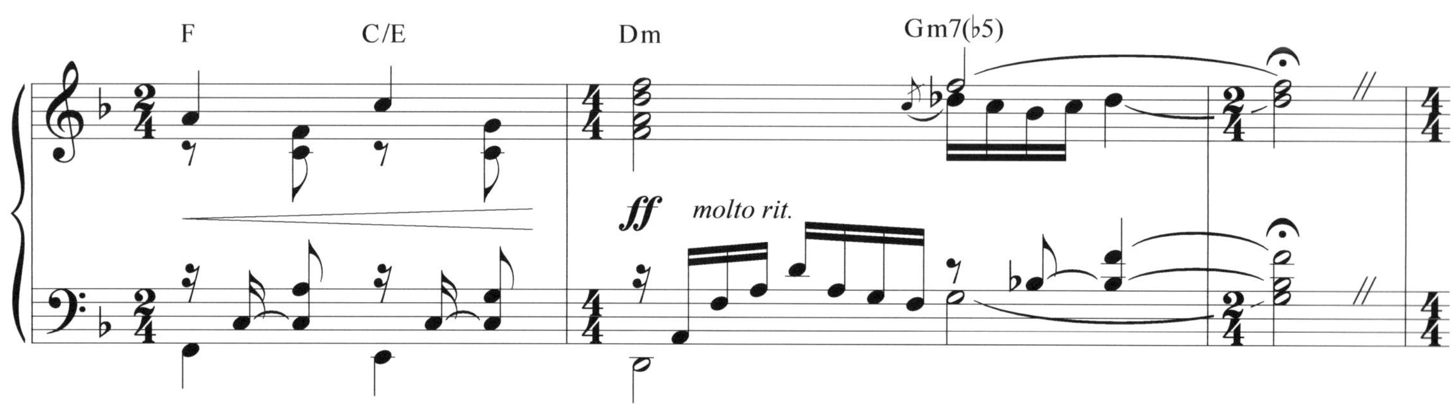
F   C/E   Dm   Gm7(♭5)
ff   molto rit.

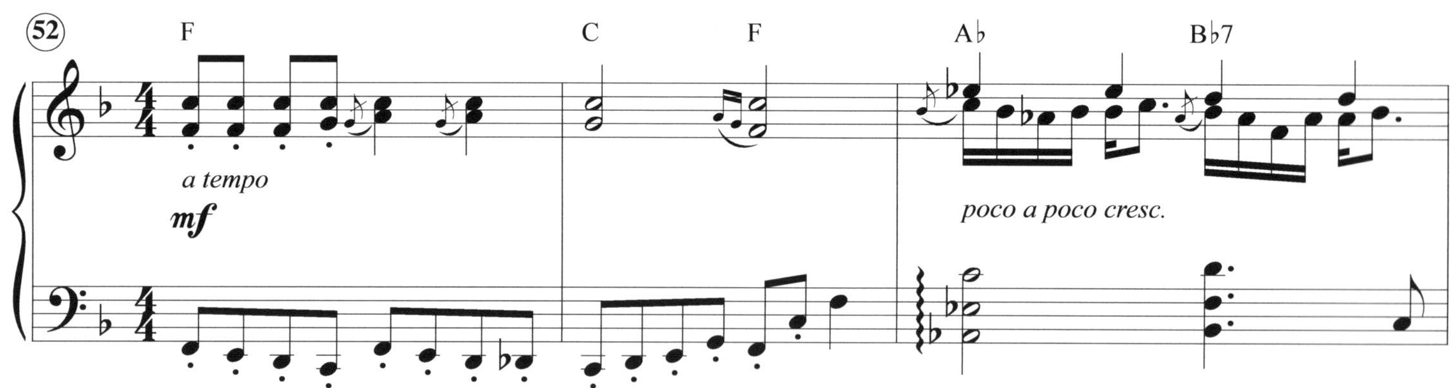
52   F   C   F   A♭   B♭7
a tempo
mf
poco a poco cresc.

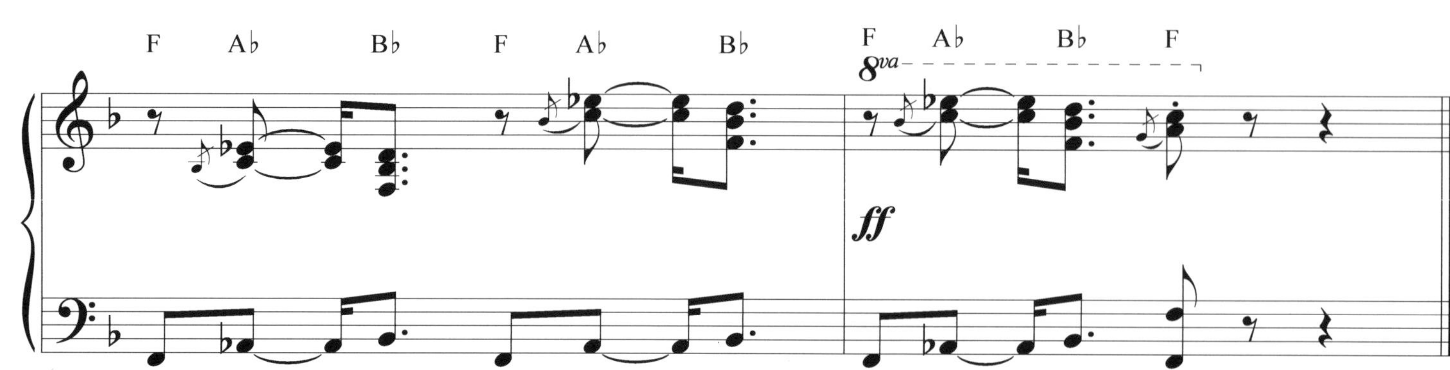
F   A♭   B♭   F   A♭   B♭   F   A♭   B♭   F
8va
ff

The Lily of the Valley

17

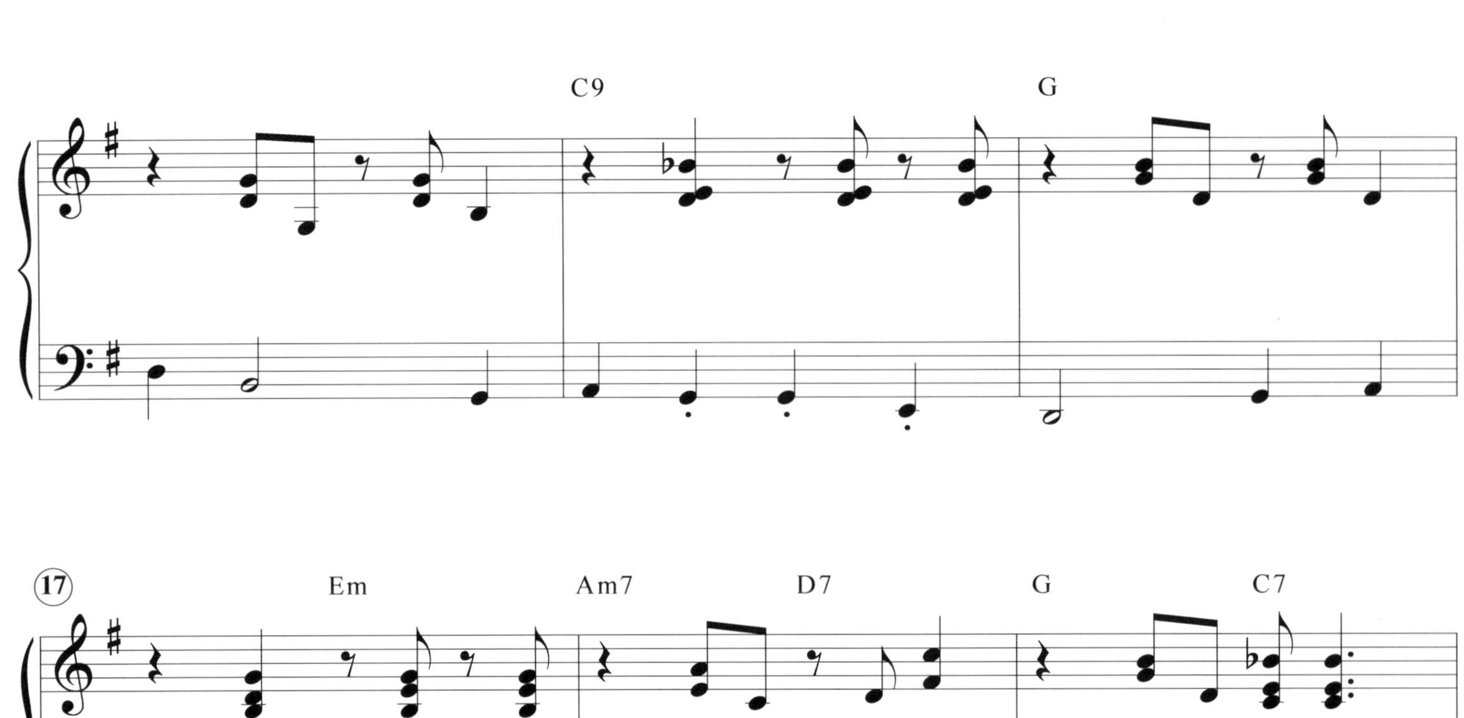

C9
G

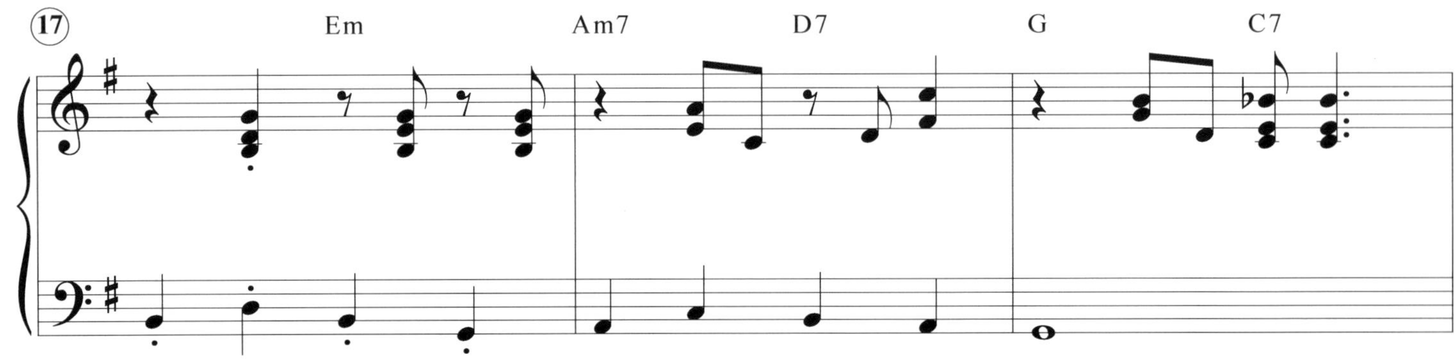

17
Em
Am7
D7
G
C7

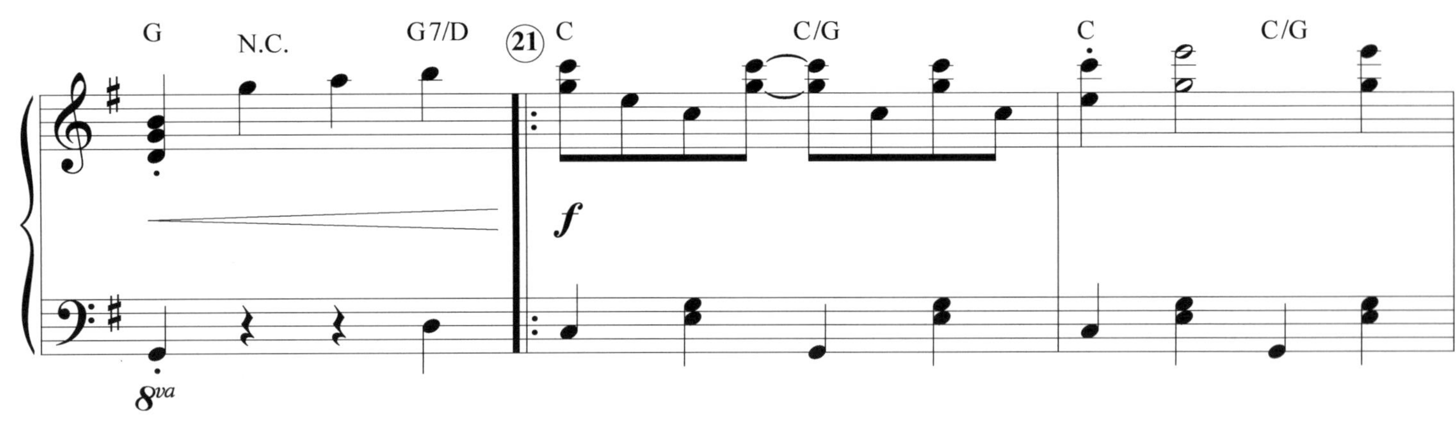

G
N.C.
G7/D
21
C
C/G
C
C/G
f
8va

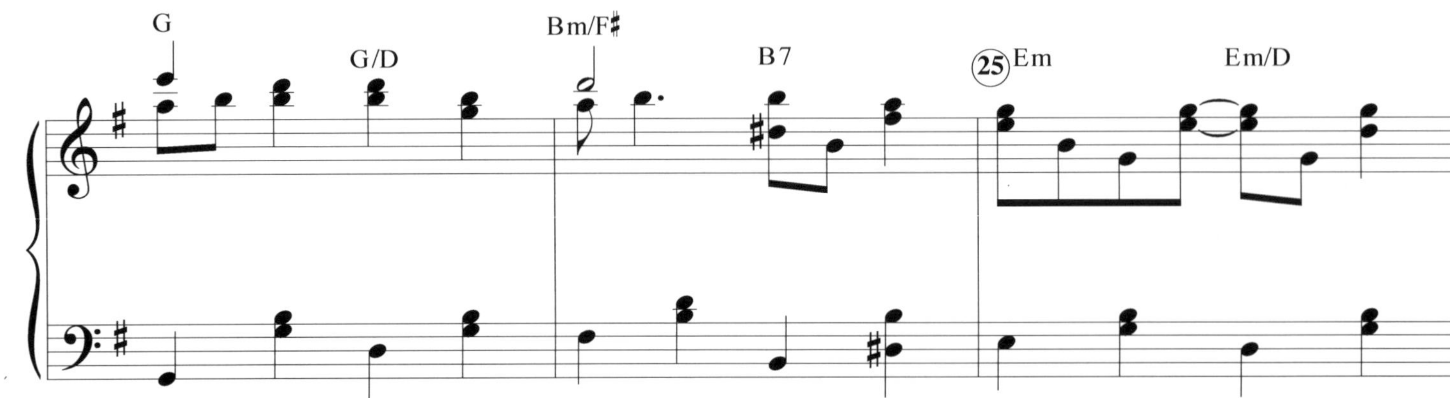

G
G/D
Bm/F#
B7
25
Em
Em/D

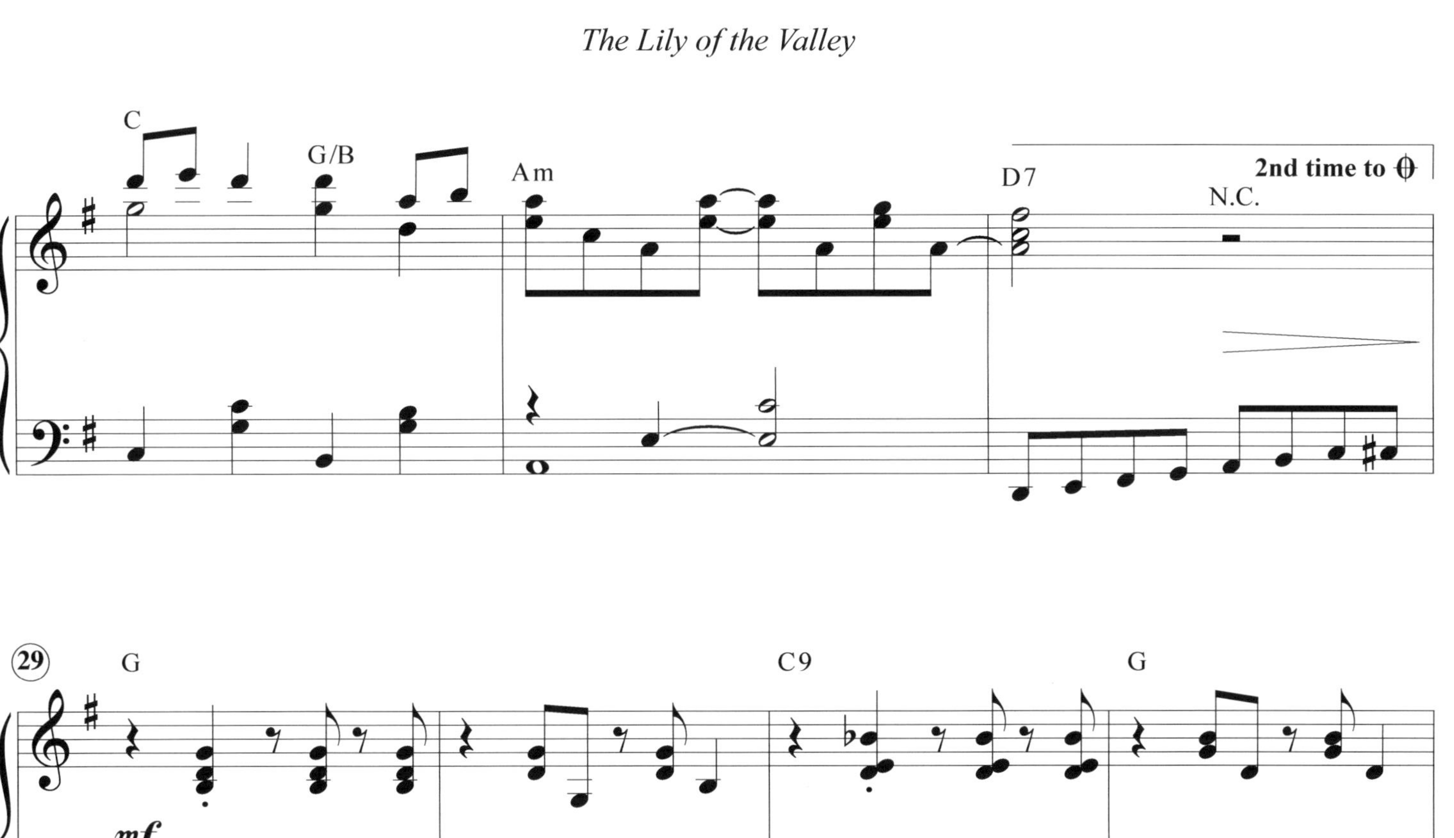
C
G/B
Am
D7
2nd time to
N.C.

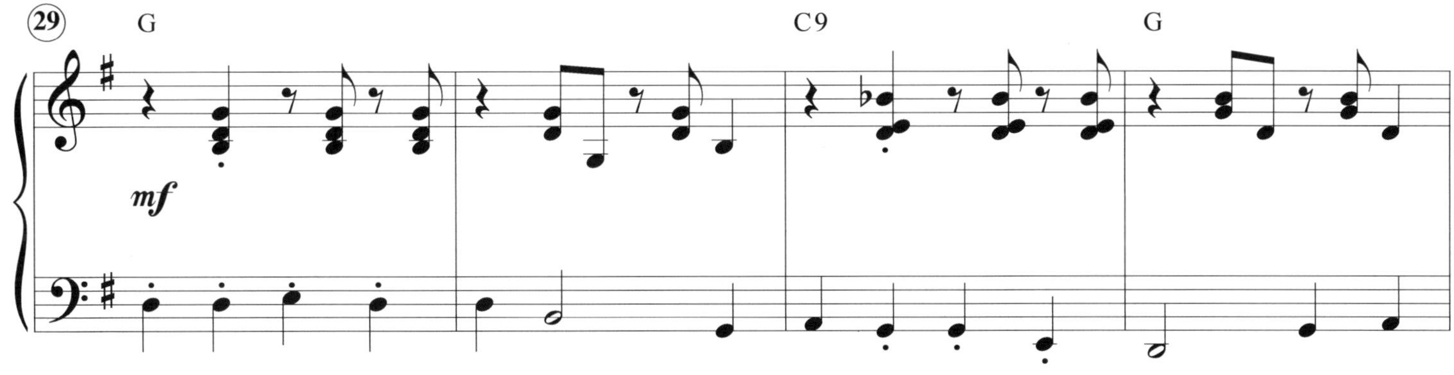
29
G
C9
G
mf

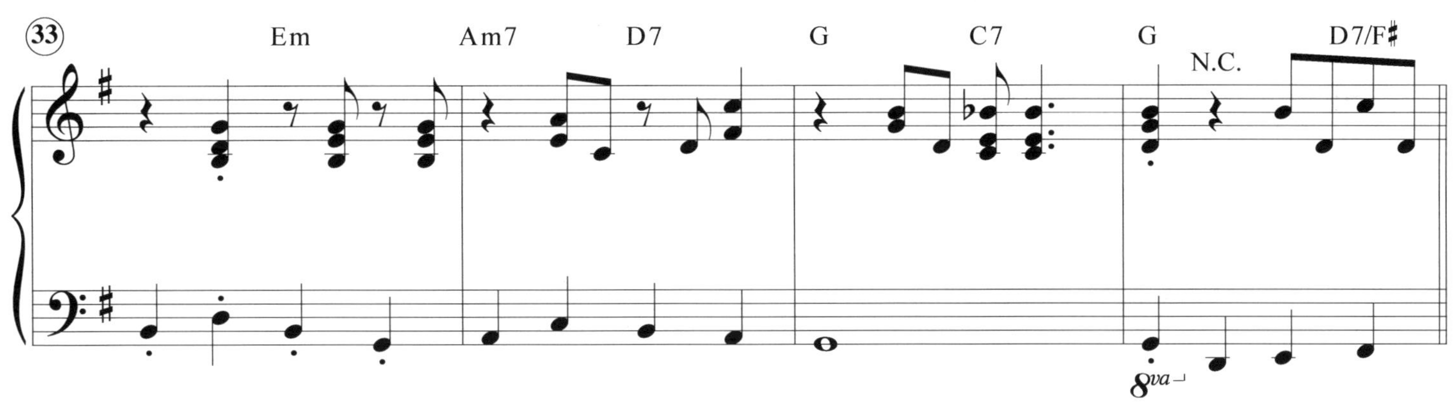
33
Em
Am7
D7
G
C7
G
N.C.
D7/F#
8va

37
G
G/D
G
C
C/G

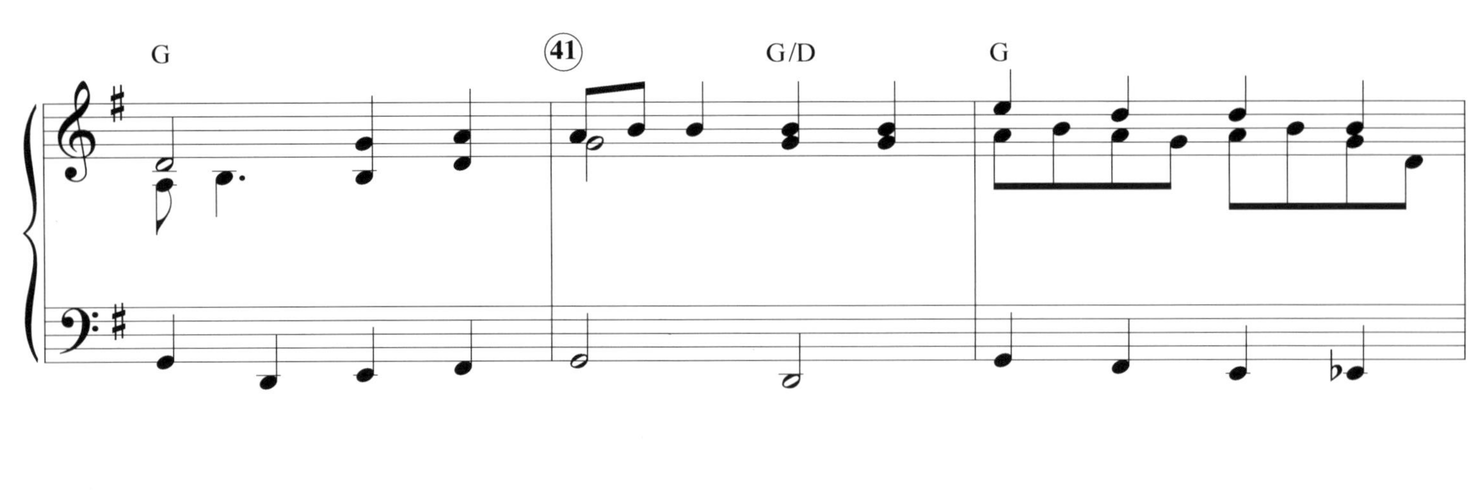

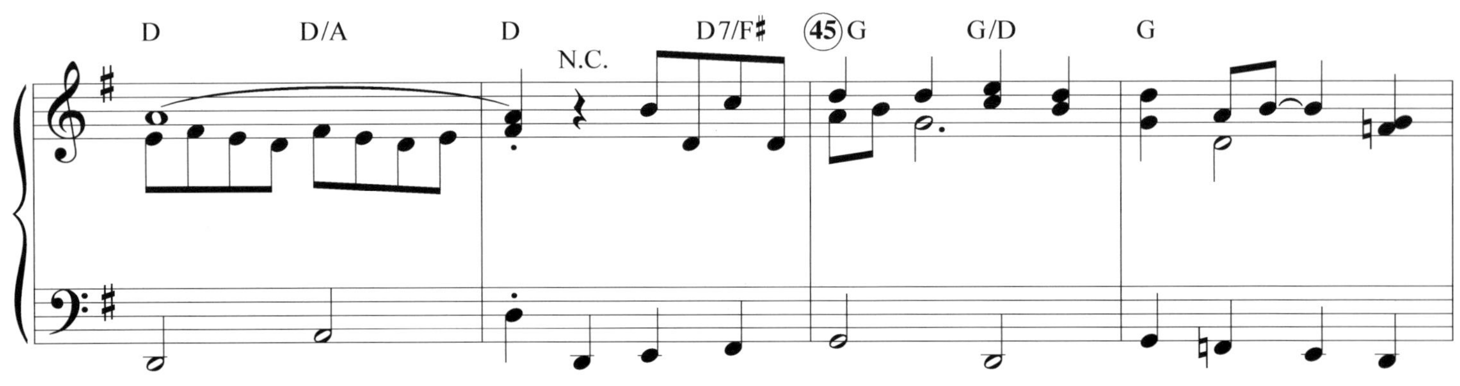

The Lily of the Valley
CODA
21

The Great Speckled Bird

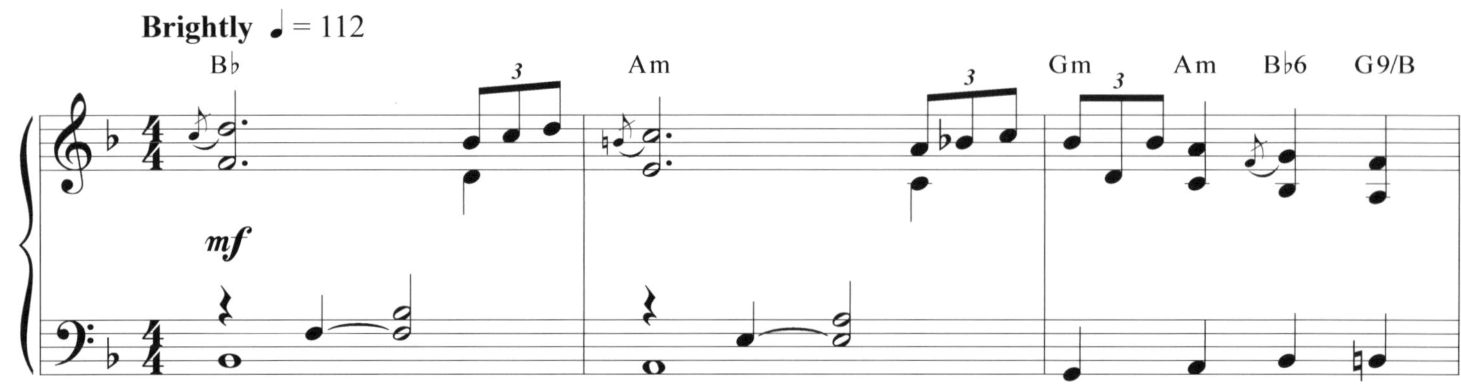

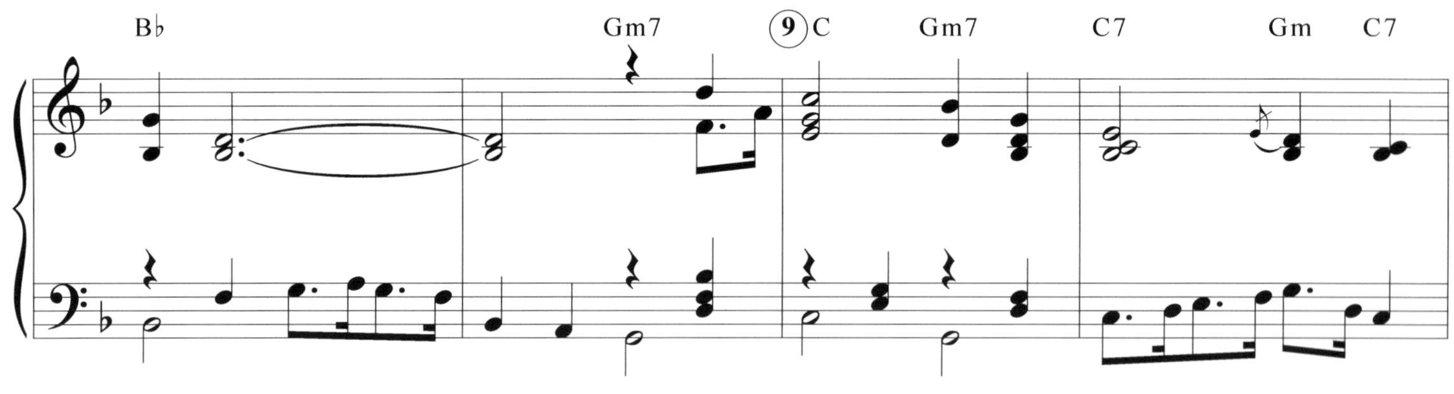

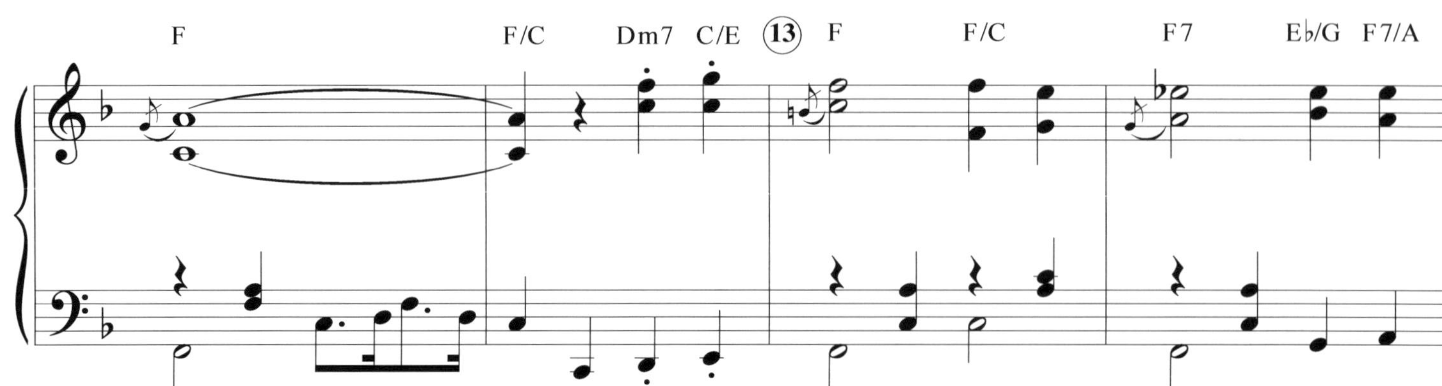

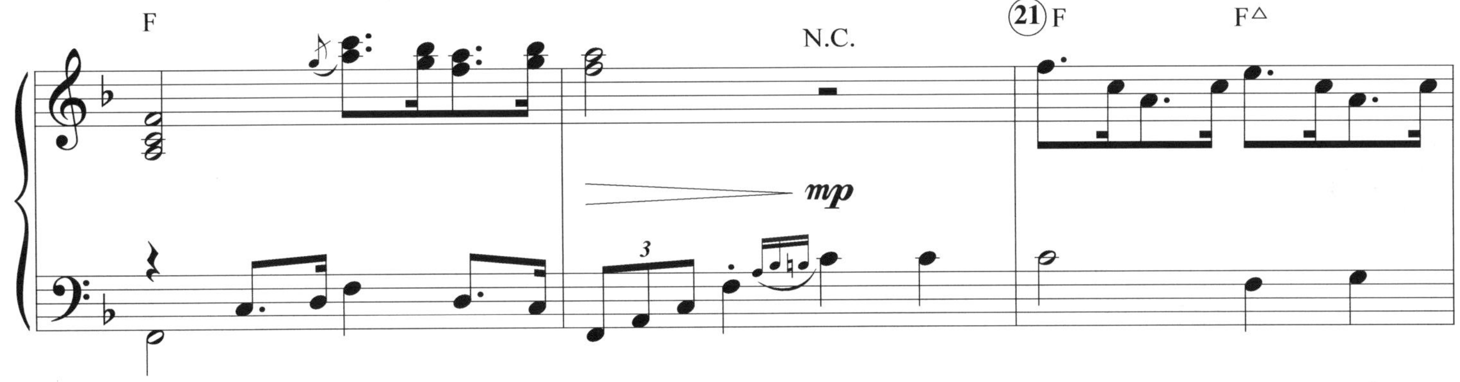

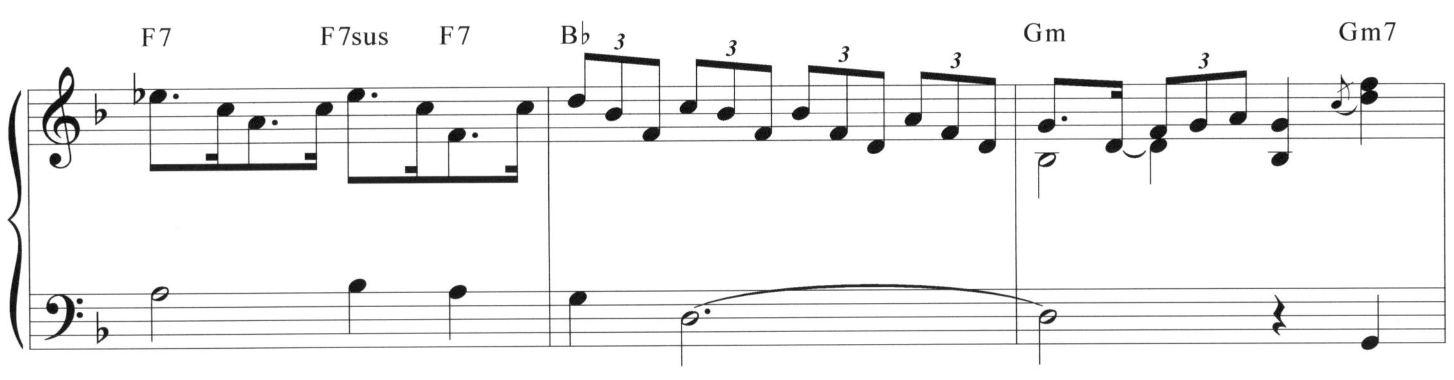

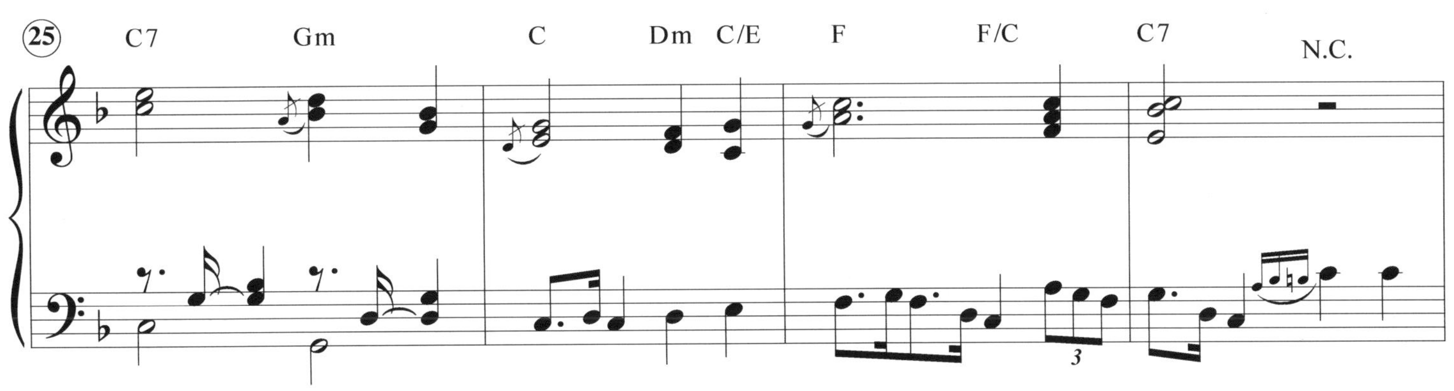

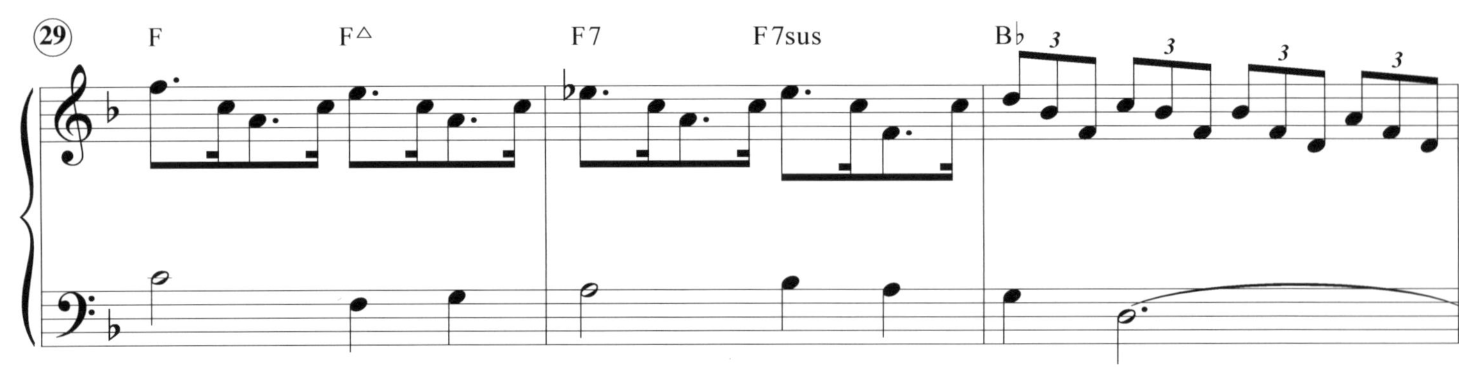

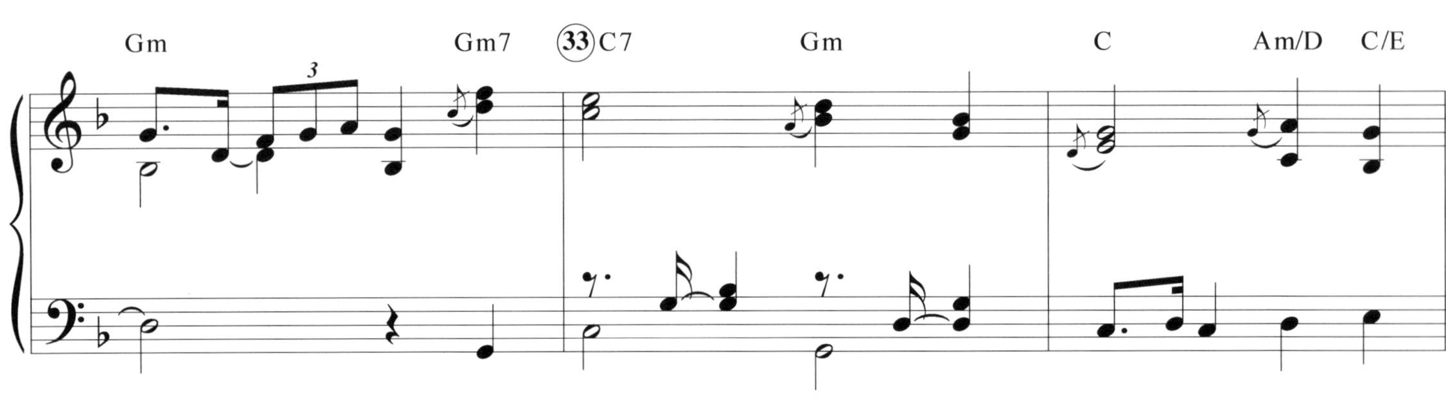

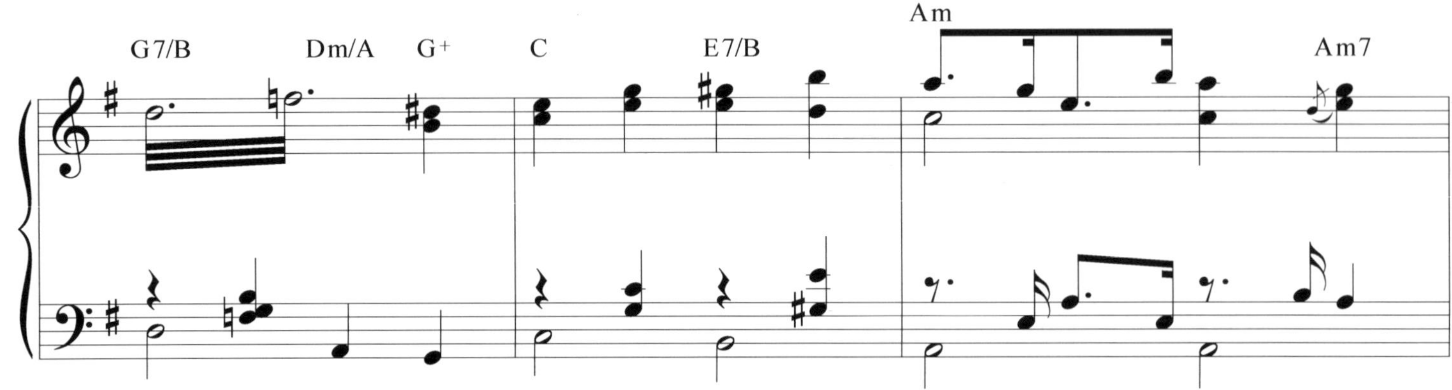

The Great Speckled Bird
41
D7
Am
D13/F#
D+
G
Em7
D7
Em7
D/F#
45
G
D/F#
G7/F
G7
Am
G7/B
C
Am7
49
D
Am
D7
Em7
D7/F#
G
G7/D
C
G
poco a poco rit.
dim.
p
25

Glory to His Name

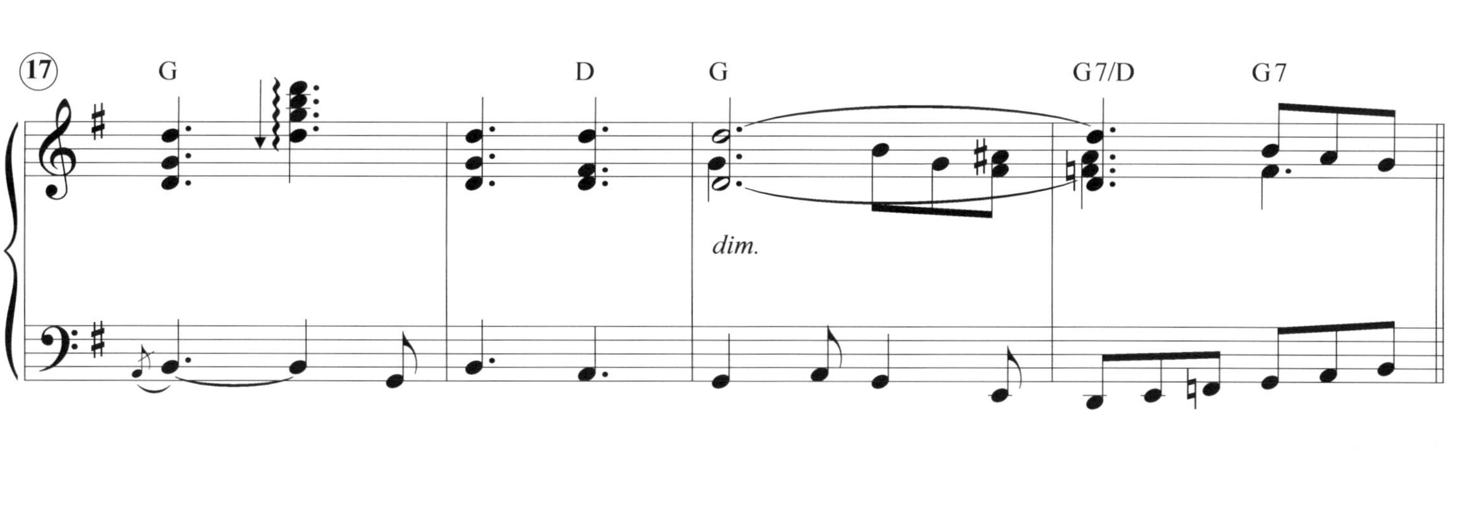

17
G
D
G
G7/D
G7
dim.

21
C
G
G/D
G
G/D
mp

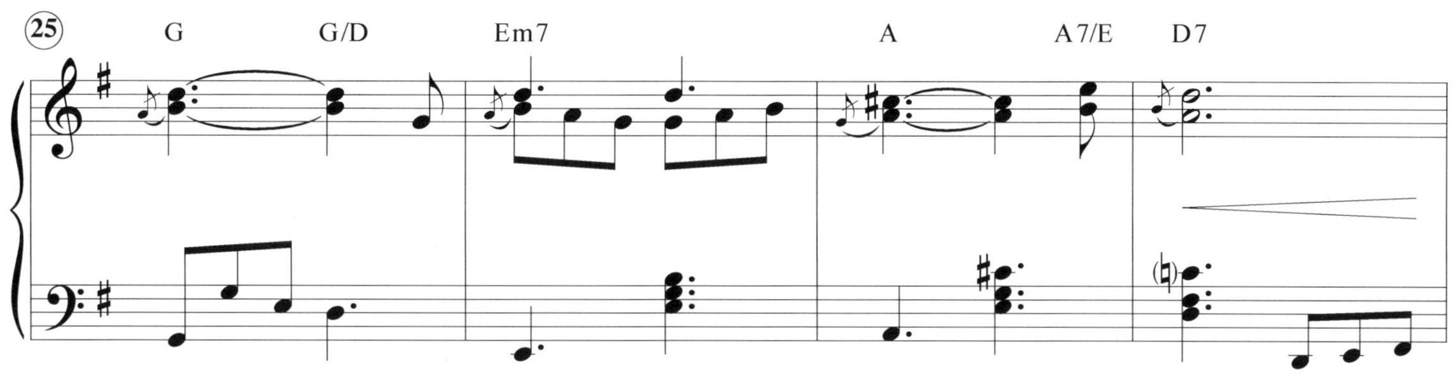

25
G
G/D
Em7
A
A7/E
D7

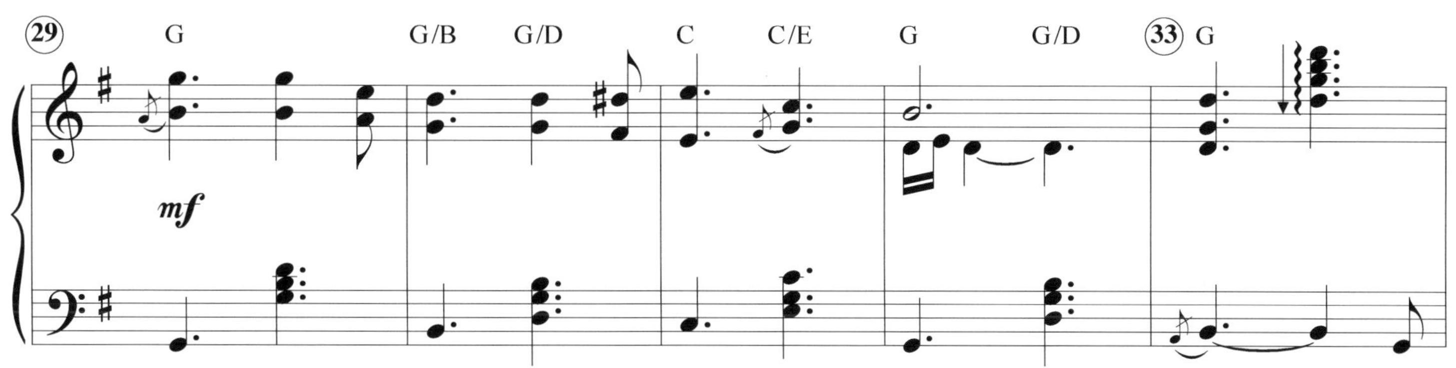

29
G
G/B
G/D
C
C/E
G
G/D
33
G
mf

D
G
E♭7
37
A♭
A♭/C
D♭
A♭
41
Cm
Fm
B♭9
E♭
E♭7
45
A♭
A♭/C
C7+
D♭
A♭
49
Fm
Cm/G
E♭7
A♭
G♭/B♭
rit. e cresc.

Ab/C
Db
53
Ab
Broader
Ab9
Eb
f
57
Fm7
Bb7
61
Eb
8va
G+
Ab
Eb
mf
65
(8va)
Eb/Bb
Eb
rit. e dim.
p
8va

Come and Dine

C. B. Widmeyer
Arr. Darrell V. Archer

C9   Gm/D C7/E   F   F/Eb   D7
17 G   G/D Dm7   G7   Dm7 G7   C
N.C.   21 G7   G7/D   Dm/G G7/A G7/B   C   C/A
C6/G   C7   25 F   A7/E   D   Em   D7/F#
mf

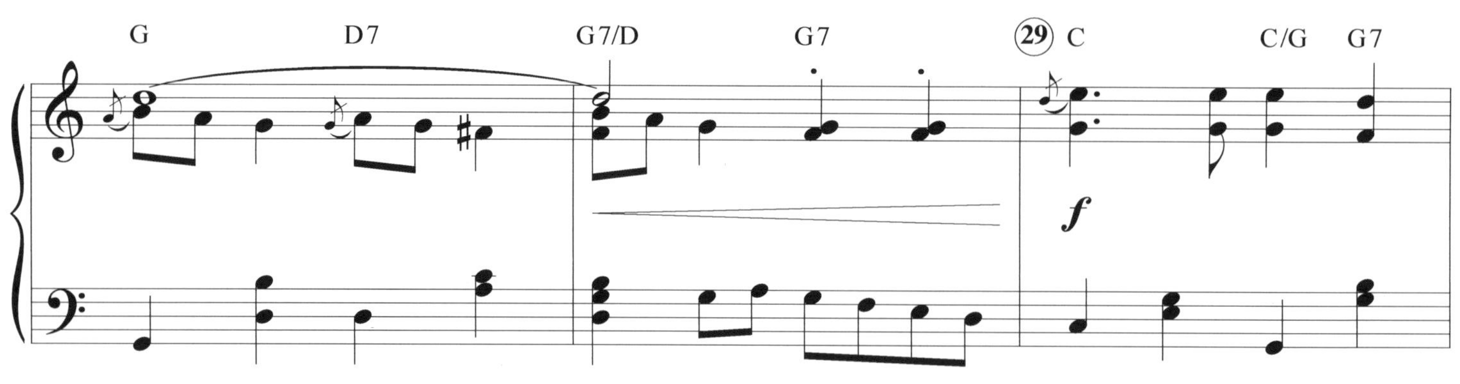

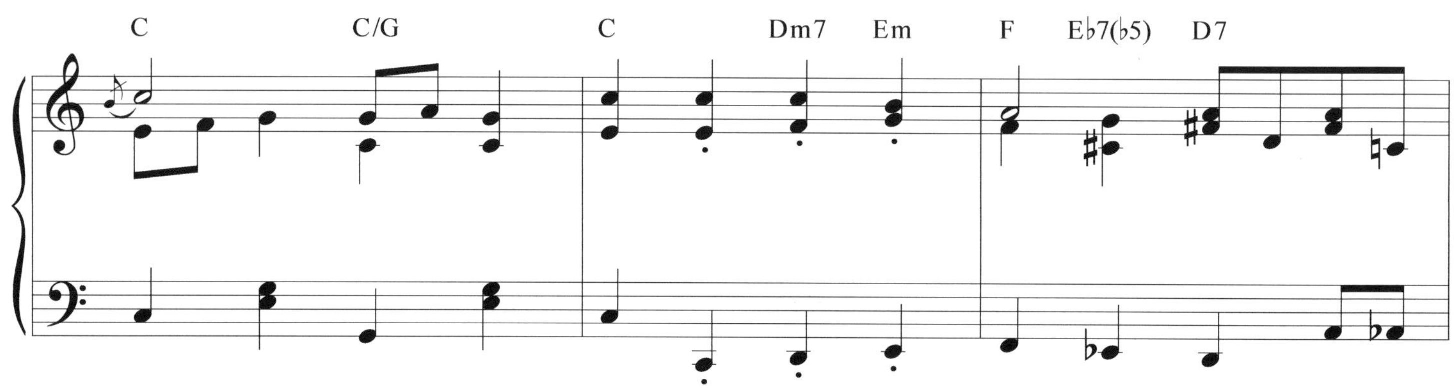

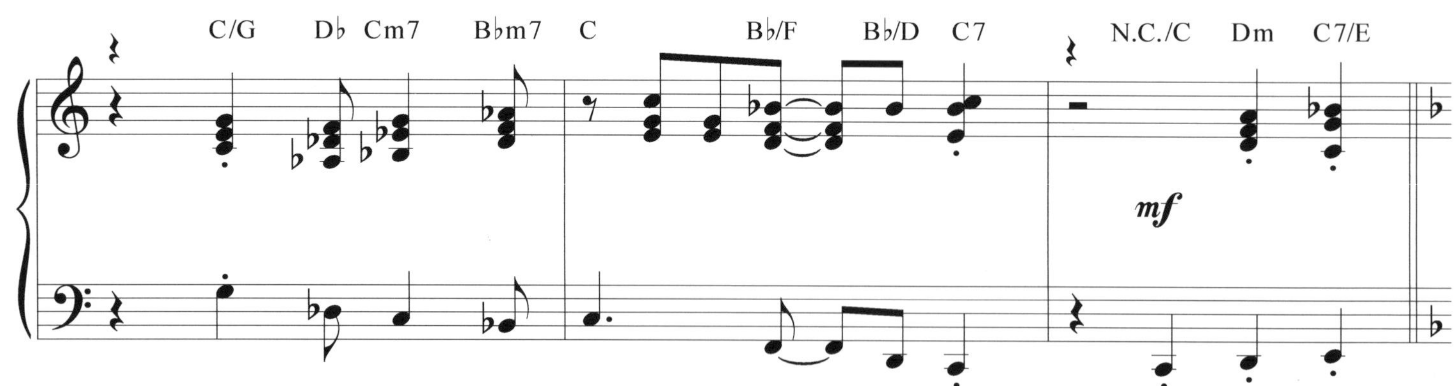

Come and Dine

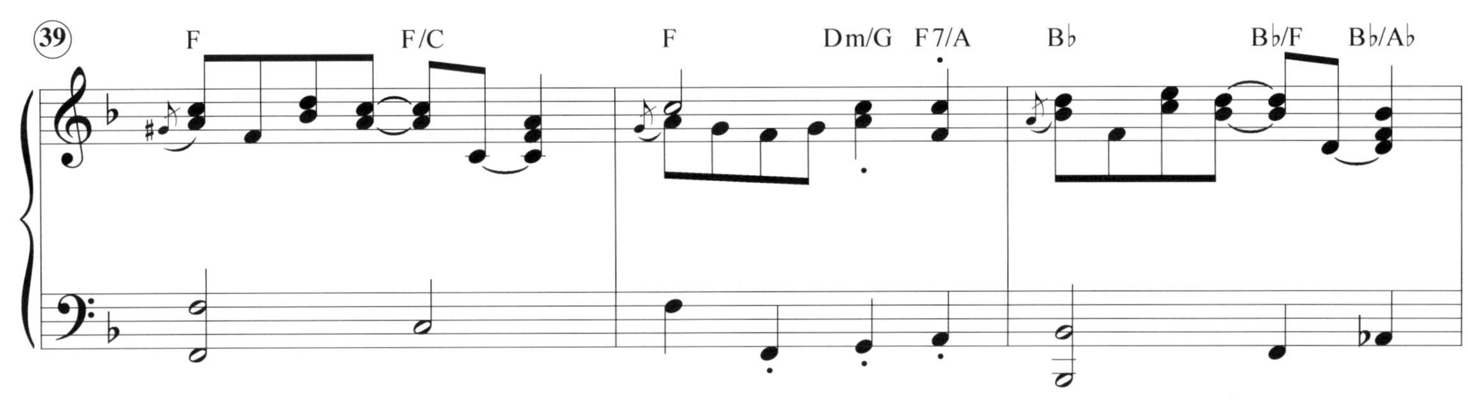

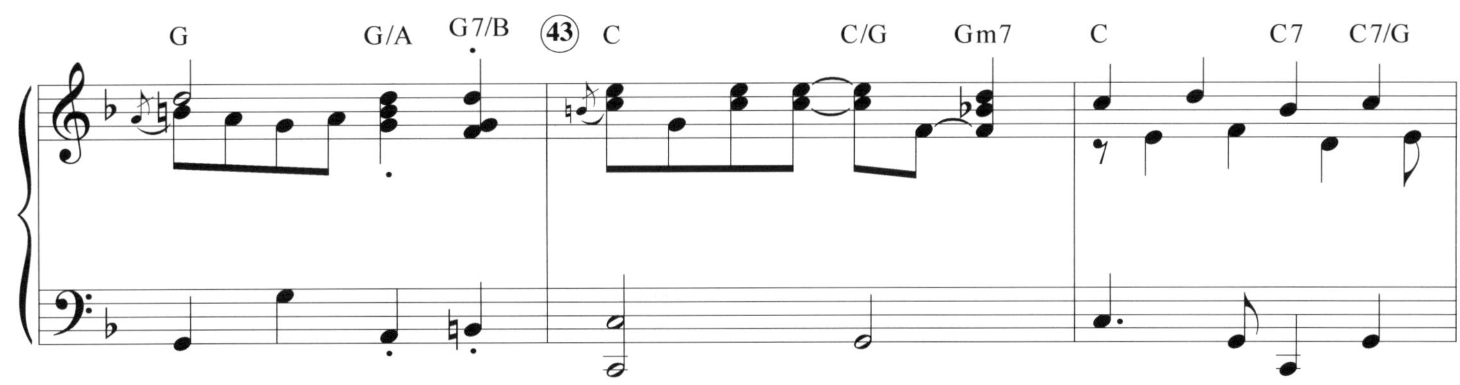

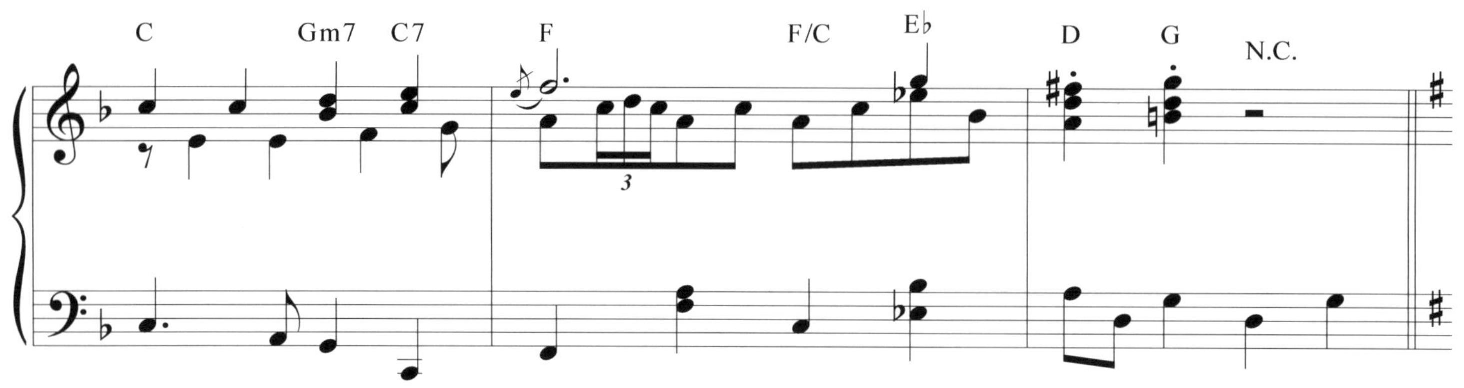

C
Gm7 C7
F
F/C
Eb
D
G
N.C.
3

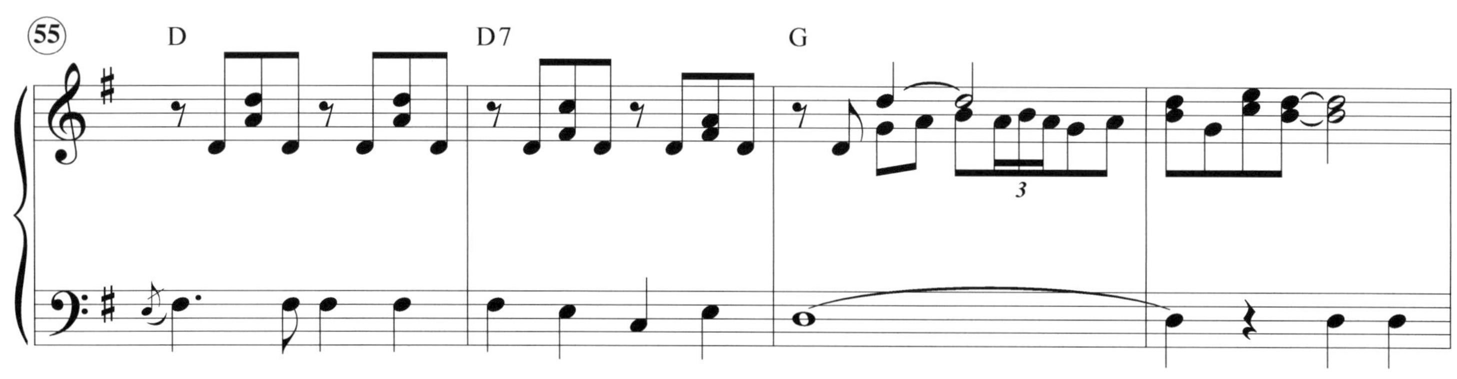

55
D
D7
G
3

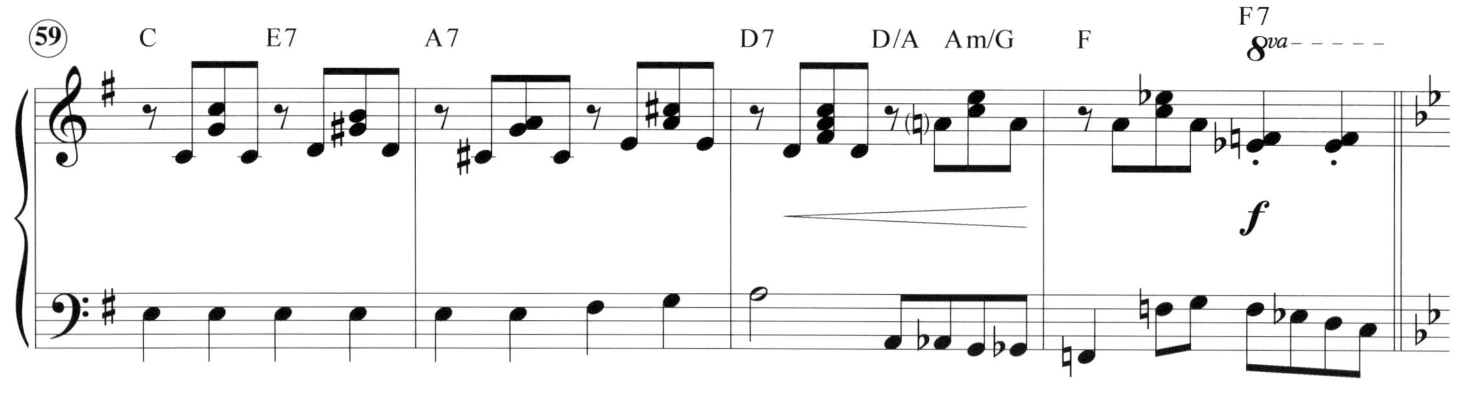

59
C
E7
A7
D7
D/A Am/G
F
F7
8va
f

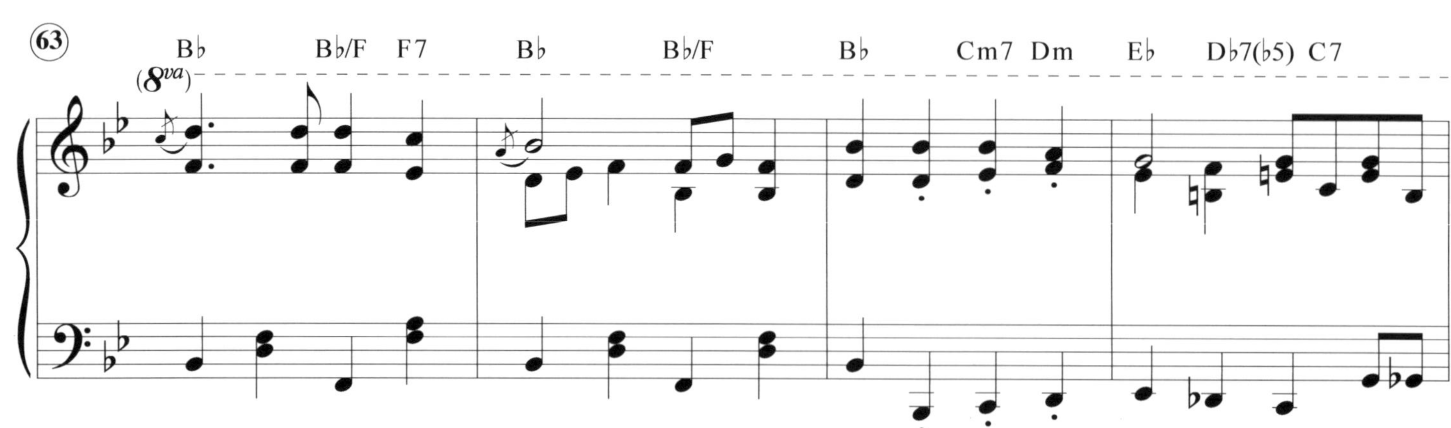

63
Bb
Bb/F F7
Bb
Bb/F
Bb
Cm7 Dm
Eb
Db7(b5) C7
(8va)

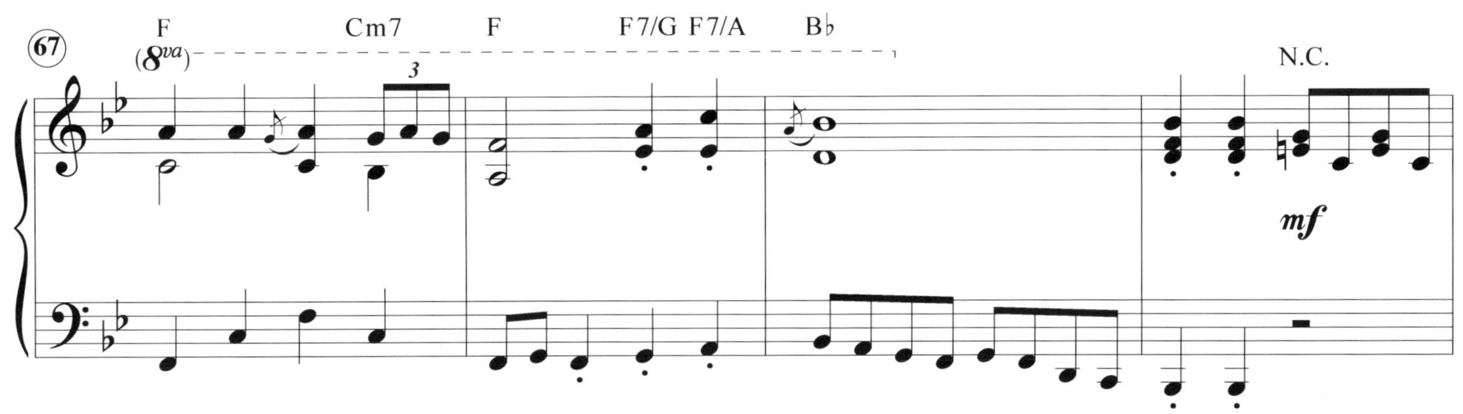

poco a poco cresc.

Peace Like a River

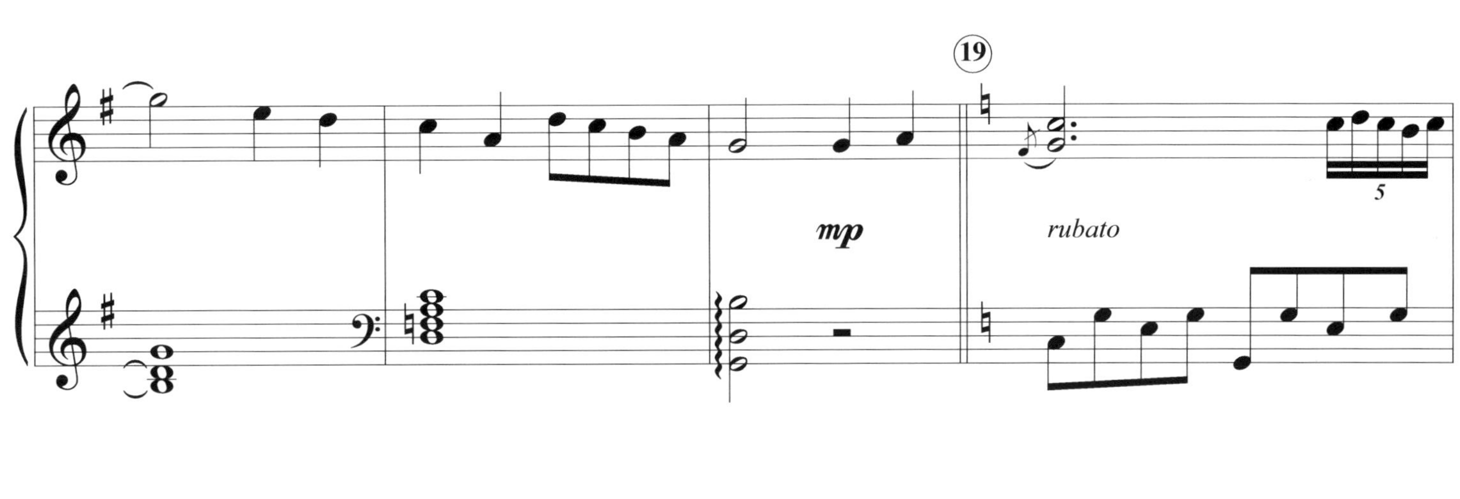
19
mp
rubato
5

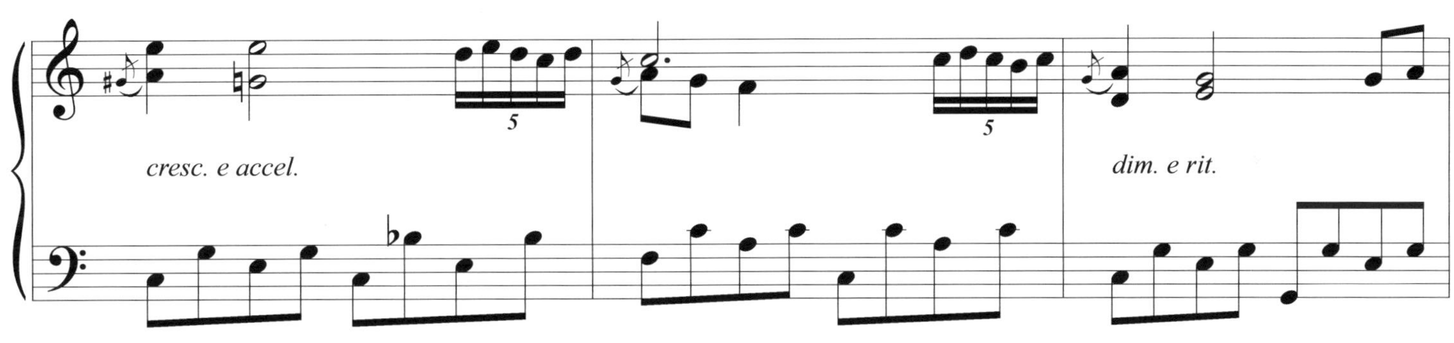
cresc. e accel.
5
5
dim. e rit.

23
5
cresc. e accel.
5

27
dim. e rit.
cresc. e accel.
5

31
dim. e rit.
mf
Easy Shuffle
mp
mf
36
F   F/C   F   A   A7/C#   Bb   Gm7   C7   N.C.
3
40
F   Dm7   F/C   G7   Em/G   G7   C   C7   C°7   Fm6/C
3   3   3

C7
N.C.
44 F
F/C
F
A
A7/C#
Bb
Gm7
C7
C7/Bb
C7/A
C7/G
48 F
Dm
G9
C7
F
E7/D
Eb7/Db
D7
N.C.
52 G
Am
f
A#°7
G/B
C7
Em7(b5)
G6
D7
3

56
G   G/F#   Em   G/D   A 7/C#   A 7/B   A 7   A 7/E   Am7sus   C 6   C#°7
D   N.C.   60 G   G/D   G7   B+
mf
C   Am   D   D7/A   64 G   G/B   Em7   Em7/B
8va
A 7   D7   G   C9   G6
(8va)   N.C.
3   3   3

68
G   G/F#   Em   Em/D   A7/C#   A7/B   A7   N.C.   D7   N.C.   G6   G6/B   G6/D   Em7
(8va)
poco a poco cresc.

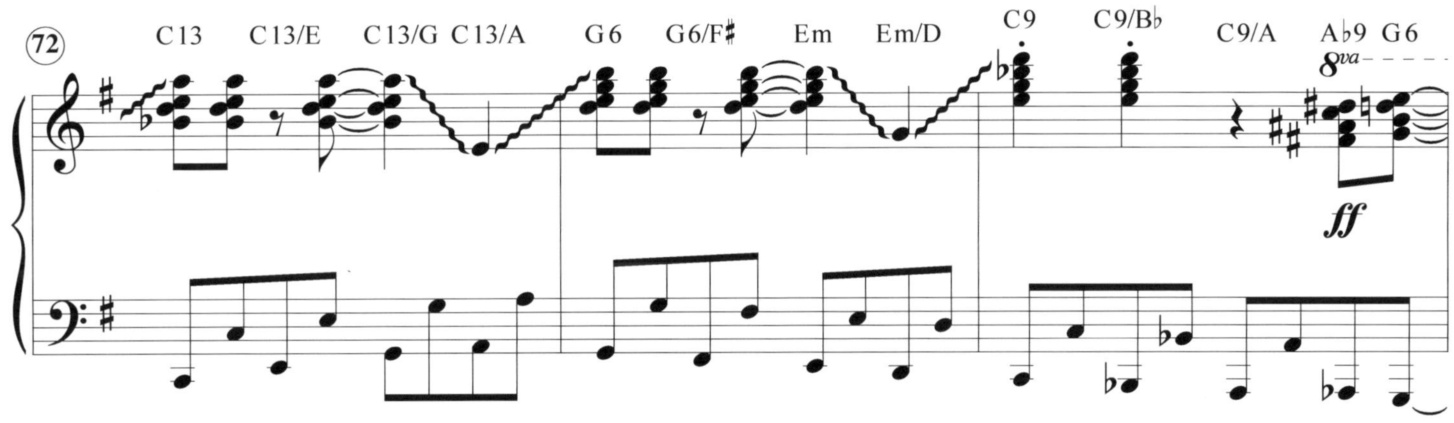

72
C13   C13/E   C13/G   C13/A   G6   G6/F#   Em   Em/D   C9   C9/Bb   C9/A   Ab9   G6
8va
ff

(8va)
N.C.   C7   C9   G6   G7(#9)   G9   G6   G7(#9)
3
N.C.
3

Unclouded Day

F
F/C
C7
32 F
F/C

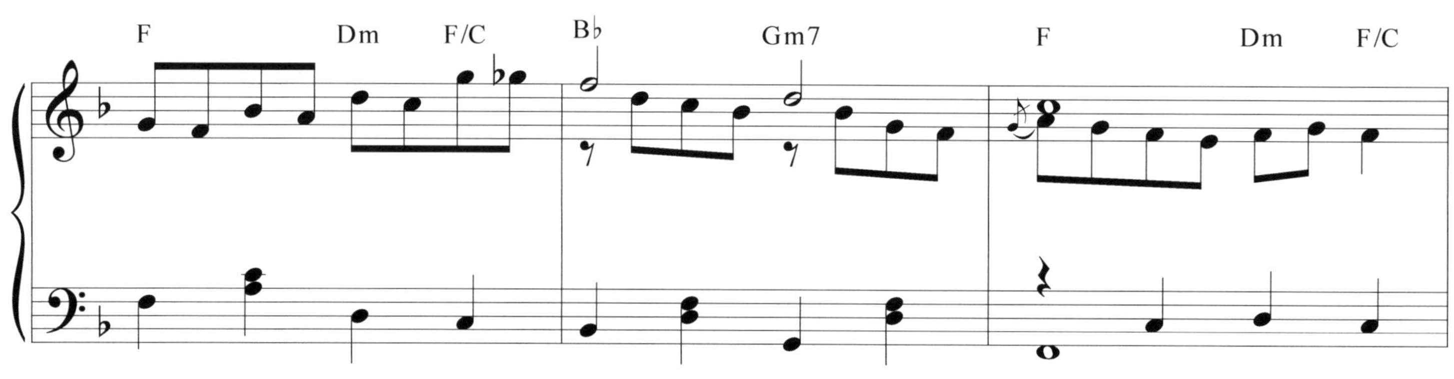
F
Dm
F/C
Bb
Gm7
F
Dm
F/C

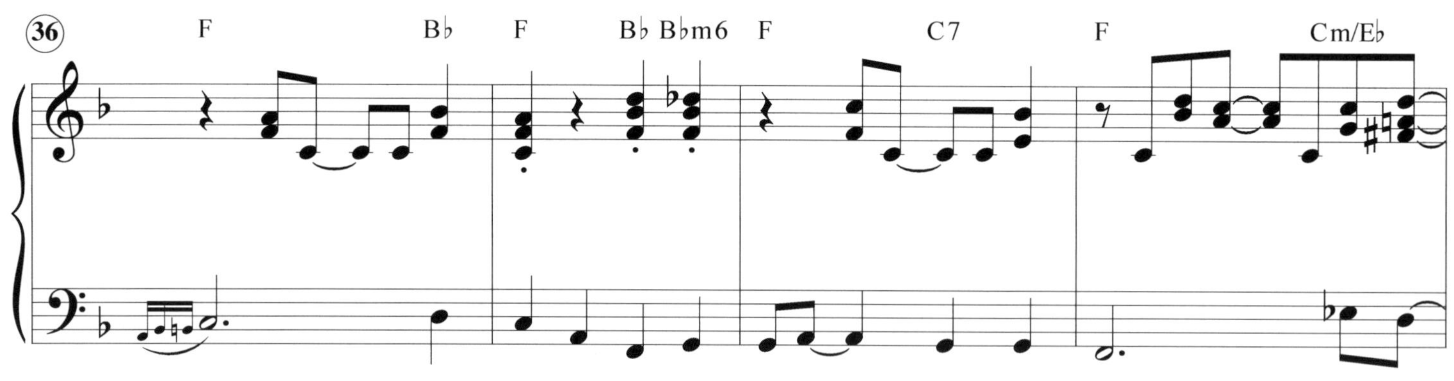
36
F
Bb
F
Bb Bbm6
F
C7
F
Cm/Eb

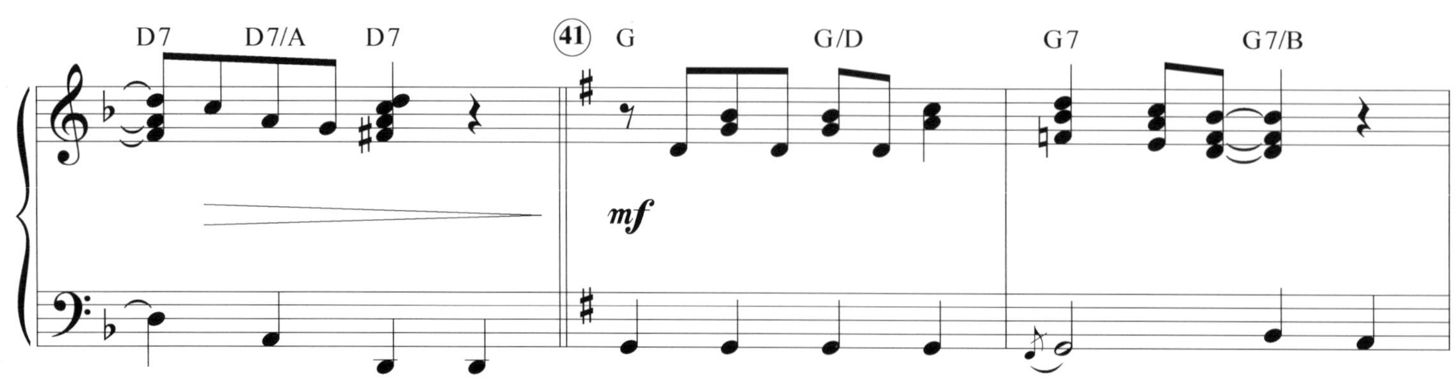
D7
D7/A
D7
41 G
G/D
G7
G7/B
mf

Unclouded Day

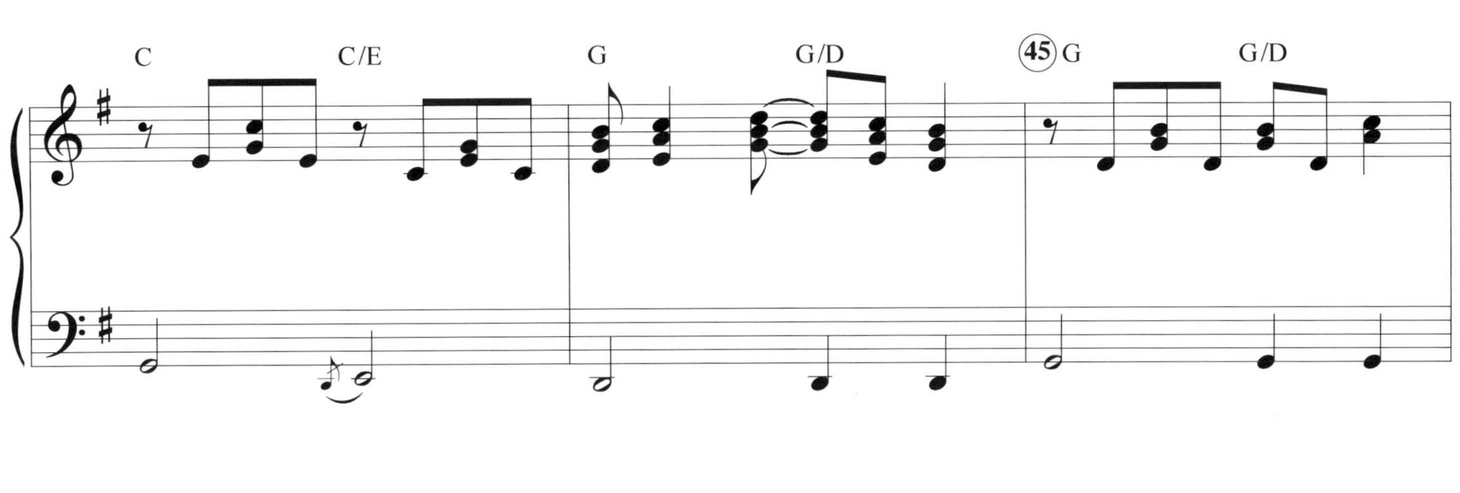

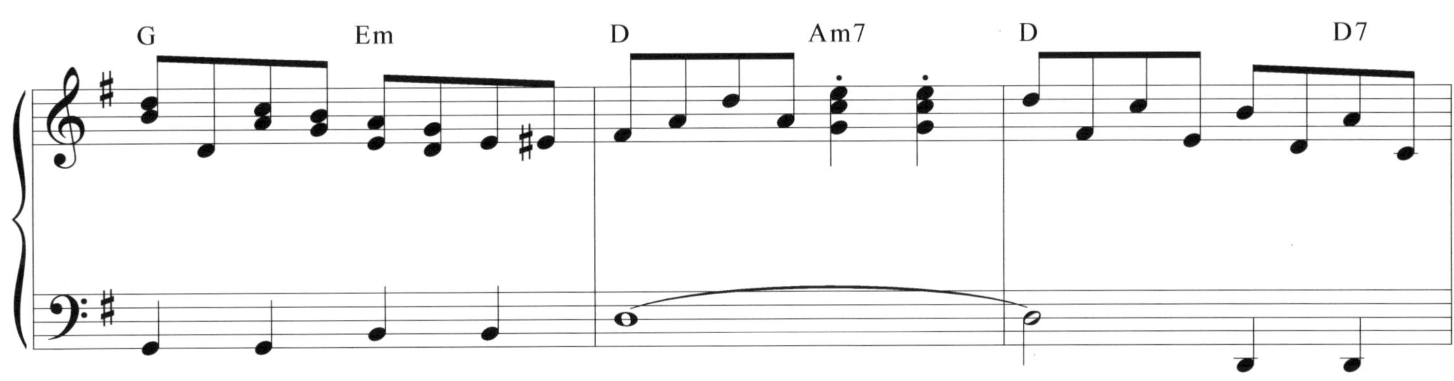

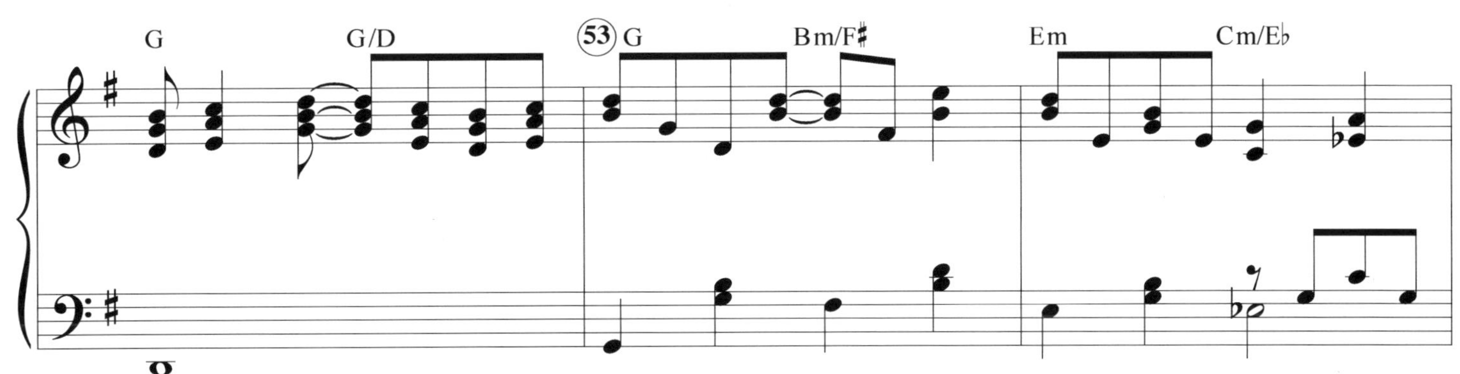

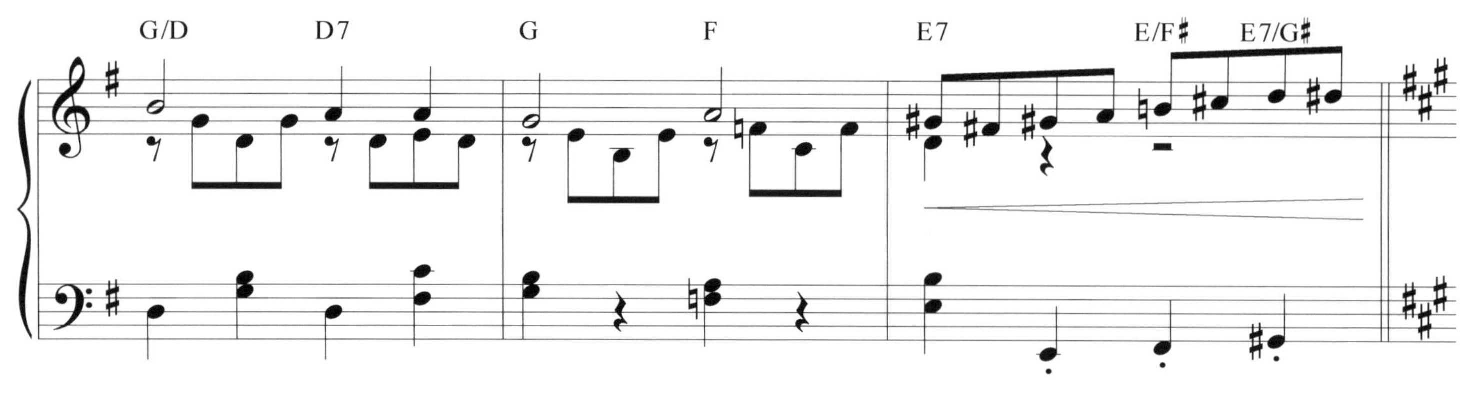

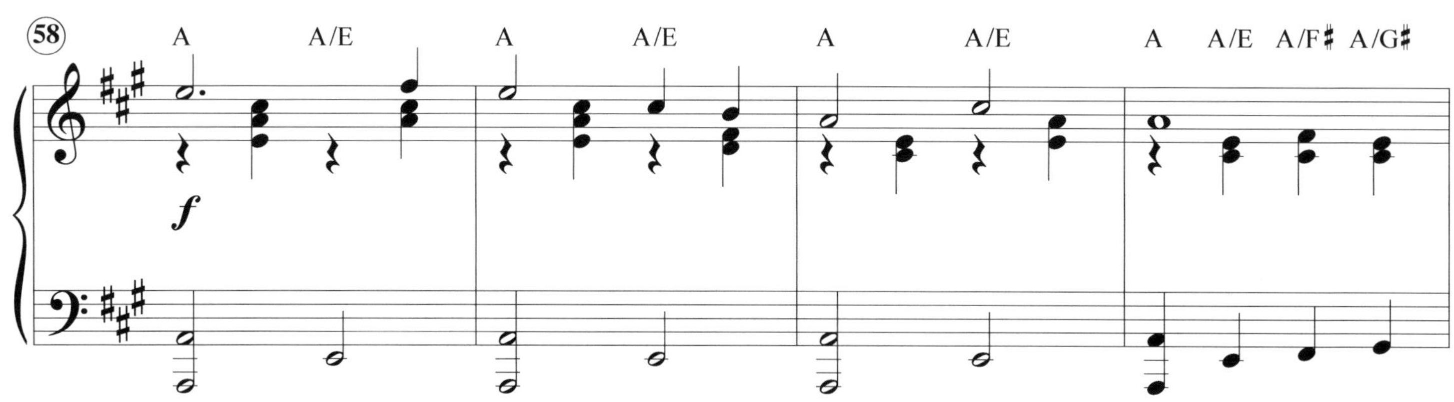

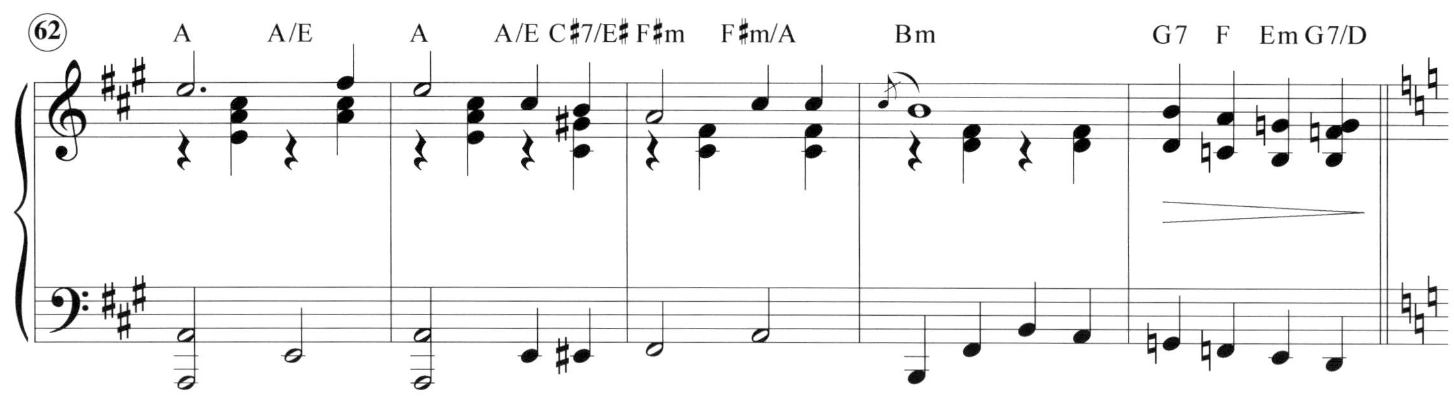

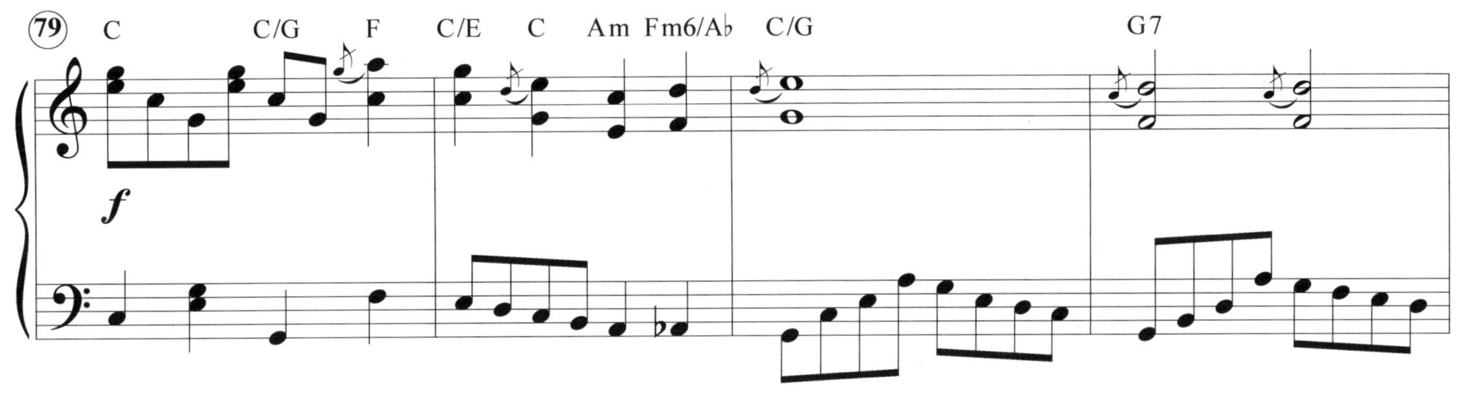

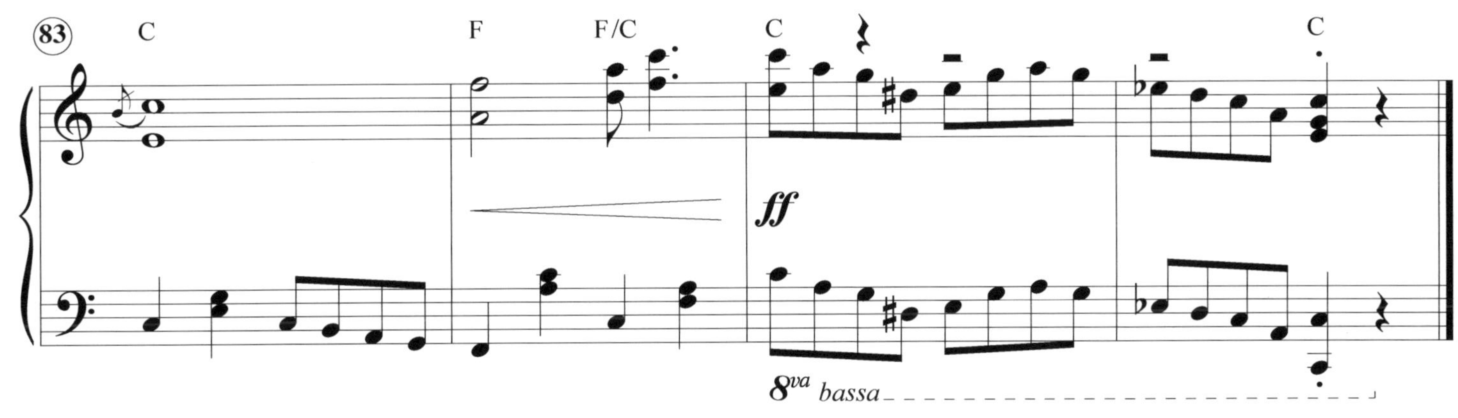

At Calvary

William R. Newell
Andante Moderato ♩ = 95
Daniel B. Towner
Arr. Darrell V. Archer
N.C.
L.H.
f
mf
G
3 C
G7/D
C/E
C
G
G7
C
F
C/E
G7/D
7 C
G7/D
C/E
C
C7+/E
F6
Dm
G7
C
Dm7
D#°7
C/E
11 F
F/E
Dm7
F/C

At Calvary
C
Em/B
Am7
C
G
G/D
G
G7
C
Dm7
D#°7
C/E
15
F
F/E
Dm7
F/C
C
Em/B
Am7
C
Dm7
G7
C
N.C.
3
3
f
mp

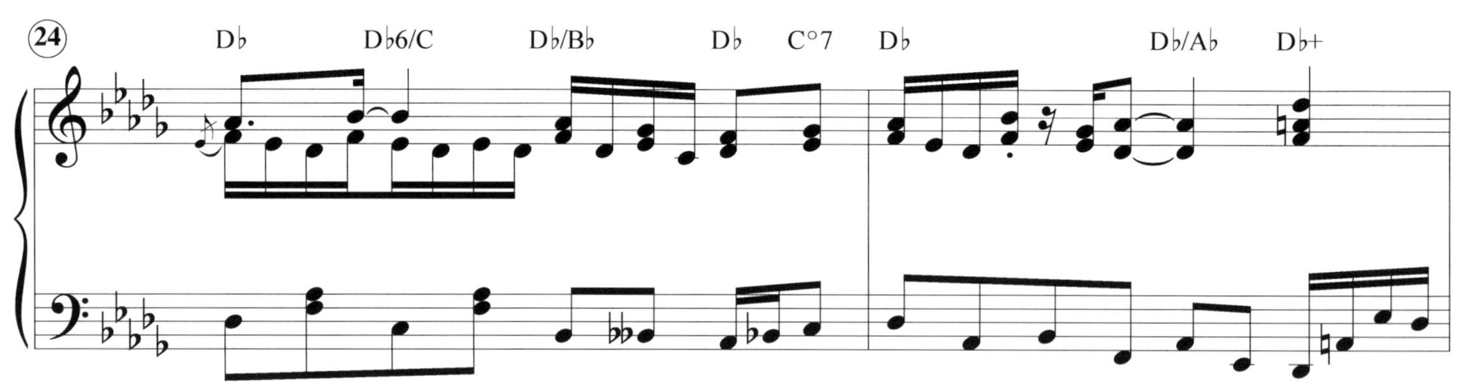

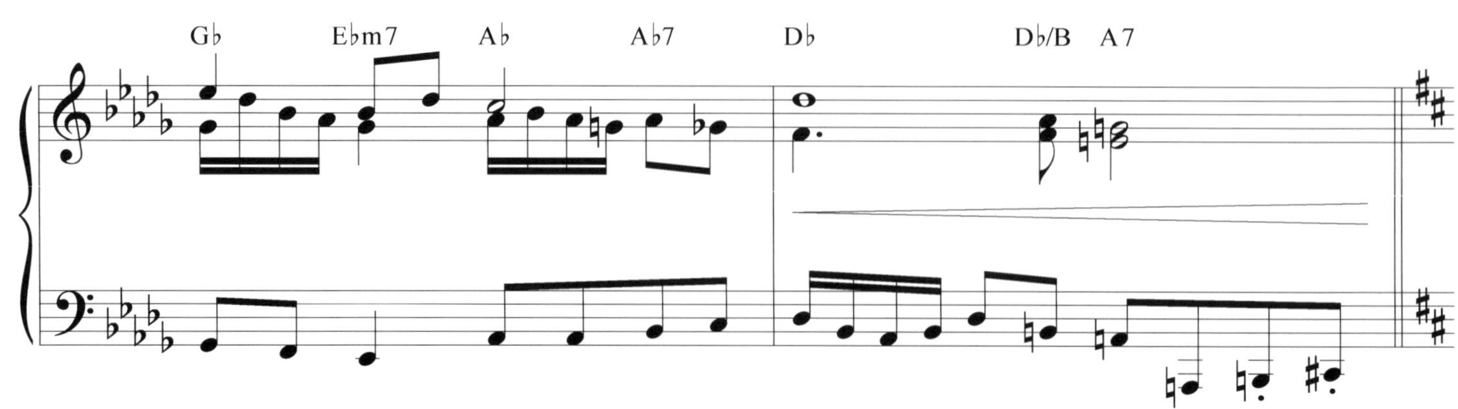

D
D/A
D
G
D
8va
mf
A
A7
D
G
D
D/A
(8va)
D
D/A
D
G
D
D+
mp
G
Em7
A
A7
D
Em7
F°7
D/A
28
32

36
G
mf
f
D△9   D6   Bm   D
A7
D△9   D6
D7
40   G
8va
Bm7/F#   Em7
G/D
f
D   D/C#   Bm7   D/A
G   Em7   A   A7
D   C   C#   D   C   C#   D   C   C#   D
p
mp
mf
ff

About the Author

Darrell Archer is a gifted composer, arranger, and pianist who has written over 2,700 pieces including orchestral arrangements, music for commercials, background music for a series of video productions, and charts for a variety of recording artists.

His individual songs, cantata, choral selections, and piano arrangements have been published by 15 different publishers and have been enthusiastically accepted and extensively used by the music buying public. Mr. Archer has previously made numerous radio and television appearances and has performed in many venues as a concert artist. He has also served as a songwriting instructor at several writer's workshops.

His abilities and vast experience have resulted in him becoming appreciated and well known as a skilled musician.

But now the righteousness of God has been manifested apart from the law, although the Law and the Prophets bear witness to it—the righteousness of God through faith in Jesus Christ for all who believe. For there is no distinction: for all have sinned and fall short of the glory of God, and are justified by his grace as a gift, through the redemption that is in Christ Jesus, whom God put forward as a propitiation by his blood, to be received by faith. This was to show God's righteousness, because in his divine forbearance he had passed over former sins. It was to show his righteousness at the present time, so that he might be just and the justifier of the one who has faith in Jesus.

Romans 3:21-26

Other Mel Bay Sacred Piano Books

10 Gospel Favorites for Piano Solo (Archer)

12 Spirituals for Piano Solo (Gail Smith)

A Classic Christmas for Piano (Gail Smith)

A Country Piano Christmas (Archer)

Christian Classics for Piano Solo (Gail Smith)

Christmas Carols for Easy Piano (Benedict)

Christmas Carols for Piano Made Easy (Gail Smith)

Classical Piano for Worship Settings (Gail Smith)

Complete Church Pianist (Gail Smith)

Country Gospel Piano Solos (Gail Smith)

Easy Piano Solos for Worship (Shirley)

Easy Way Christmas Song Folio/Piano (S. Banks)

English Carols for Piano Solo (Gail Smith)

Favorite Hymns for Piano Solo (T. Price)

Favorite Hymns to Play for Piano (Leytham)

Gospel Piano Made Easy (Gail Smith)

Hymns Made Easy for Piano Book 1 (Gail Smith)

Hymns Made Easy for Piano Book 2 (Gail Smith)

Hymns Made Easy for Piano Book 3 (Gail Smith)

If Snowmen Could Make Music (Benedict)

Music is for Everyone Christmas Book Level 1: For Young Children (Gilbert)

Old-Time Gospel Piano (Cummings/Whitmire)

Praise Piano Made Easy (Gail Smith)

Preludes and Offertories for Piano Solo (Gail Smith)

Wedding Music for Piano (T. Price)

WWW.MELBAY.COM